ON TH_

If you don't love this . . . you just plain don't love dancing!

By: Dennon Rawles

Co-conspirator: Sayhber Rawles

Original Artwork and Illustrations: Matthew Alan Rawles

Graphic Design: Ashley Rae Bergin

Digital Artist: Bethany Tidwell

Edited by: Stacy Effron Taylor

Dedicated to My Jessica

Photo: Steven Thomas

"The Perfectly Executed Tendu"
by
Jessica Terese Rawles

There she stood.
Feet resisting against the filthy, cold,
yet inviting floor beneath her.
Her torso lifting up in the opposite direction
trying to prove physics amiss.

Her strong ankles lifted up proud
demanding the respect of royalty,
as her feet pressed through the floor.

Her heel inched forward as the energy of the opposite pull
extended slowly into her leg.

Her articulate foot, like smooth honey, peeled off the floor
as it extended away from her.

Further and further her leg extended from her body
with so much energy, it was as if a bolt of lightening
were zapping all the way through the tip of her toes.

Then, right back into the floor and up through her body again.
For it was her instrument and only source of power.

And after, proud of her work, she got ready to do it again.
For it was her life.

"But what did she do?" the layman asked.
"A perfectly executed tendu", I answered smiling.
"For only a few people know the amount of energy it takes
to perform the most simple task in a daily routine
when it is done correctly."

ON THE FLOOR

If You Don't Love This . . . You Just Plain Don't Love Dancing!

Contents

Photo: Paul Da Silva

PREFACE
WHY I'M COMPELLED TO WRiTE THiS BOOK
"NOW DO IT LiKE THAT!"

"When I was your age . . . I was much younger!" The year was 1974, and I was in great need of a job . . . a real honest-to-goodness, money-paying job. At the time, I had been training and dancing with the Los Angeles-based Steven Peck Jazz Company doing some pretty demanding concert work. Because it was a concert company, the pay was nil. What money I did make was primarily from teaching. I remember thinking I should have been paid better for all the grueling, demanding, downright painful late-night hours we were putting in. As the years passed by though, I realized that I was paid! The marvelous training I received during my tenure there has paid dividends many times over.

One of the most important lessons I learned had to do with the concept of "paying dues". My dues were paid over a five-year period, dancing for a dance master who related as much, if not more, to his Sicilian heritage as he did to the art, craft and discipline of dance. Boy did I learn a lot in those days. Still, I found myself increasingly in need of money. No doubt about it, it was time to take that training, experience and knowledge I gained and put it to the test.

The audition was for the Academy Awards Show. In recent years, the Oscars have done little to lessen the unemployment rate of dancers, but back then it was one of the most coveted "commercial" dance jobs of the year. It was through this experience that I learned a very important distinction. Whereas "concert" most often means technically challenging, artistically and creatively fulfilling work, "commercial" means . . . it means . . . well let's face it, it means money. Don't get me wrong, commercial work can also be technically challenging, and artistically and creatively fulfilling, but it's just . . . well, it can often be mundane and at times just plain silly. So what are my choices? Artistically fulfilling work or . . . money? I wanted, no, I needed to pay my rent, so I decided to try "commercial".

Let me set the scene. The audition was to be held at the old, and I do mean old, Falcon Studios in Hollywood. A 1928 and 1932 Olympic Fencing Team member Ralph Faulkner, and his wife Edith Jane, a Ballet instructor, ran this historic fencing and dancing academy. In the early days of movies, Mr. Faulkner taught and coached many actors on the art of fencing. The atmosphere of this large dusty, musty studio was eerie to say the least. There were these ancient photos lining the long hallway walls boasting of its famed students. There was Errol Flynn, Douglas Fairbanks, Jr., Tyrone Power, Basil Rathbone, and a bunch of others from that time period thrusting and parrying their little swash-buckling hearts out. In the back of the main multi-roomed studio, separated by a rather charming albeit unkempt garden area, was a large barn-shaped studio, about the size of an airplane hanger. You could smell, feel and, if you squinted hard enough, see the ghosts of dancers past.

The choreographer was two-time Tony Award winner, Ron Field—a rather scary fellow known for his intimidating manner. He was a former Jack Cole dancer (talk about scary—more about him later) who had choreographed and directed such Broadway shows as *Cabaret* and *Applause*. I didn't really know all that much about him at the time. I just knew he was a well-established Broadway guy, which was pretty impressive to this naive young man.

Liza Minnelli was set to be the star performer. Wow, Liza Minnelli! She was at the top of her game. She was a Tony winner for *Flora, the Red Menace*, and an Oscar winner for the film *Cabaret* and, to top it off, her recent TV Special, *Liza with a Z* was awarded an Emmy. I was excited, to say the least. Who wouldn't be? It was sure to be a good-paying job that featured superstar Liza Minnelli, all choreographed by "Broadway guy" Ron Field.

There must have been close to a hundred and fifty guys there, maybe more. (I could be exaggerating, but it sure seemed that way.) As new at this game as I was, and I was, even I knew they didn't need that many guys. I felt, and I'm sure we all felt, the pressure to do our best. The assistant choreographers began teaching us the audition combination. There we all were, on the floor, a very crowded floor, working extremely hard . . . all jockeying for the best positions to be noticed.

It all seems so silly to me now that, whether it be an audition or in everyday dance class, "being noticed" seems to be a major concern. I've since learned it is a misguided notion to be right up front and in the face of those in charge in order to be noticed. Oh it's good to be noticed, especially at auditions, but here's the thing . . .

THiNG # 1

THE GOOD WiLL BE NOTiCED . . . WHEREVER THEY ARE!

If you're good, interesting, exciting, dynamic and, sometimes just as important, a tad on the cute side, YOU WILL BE NOTICED! The good (talented, well-trained, charismatic) dancer cannot be hidden no matter where he or she is positioned on the floor, and the bad dancer also cannot hide no matter where he or she stands. The mediocre dancer, on the other hand, can hardly be found.

Listen up, if you're ready and have what the choreographer needs, wants, and deems important for what he or she intends, do not concern yourself about pushing your way to the front—you will be spotted!

Now, back to the story. There I am at my very first television audition, nervous as can be, dancing my little heart out in desperate hope of landing an actual money-paying job. I'm doing everything I can to be noticed. (I hadn't yet learned THING # 1.)

I'm amazingly intent and equally intense. My throttle is out all the way, I'm in high gear and my pedal is definitely to the metal. Now understand, "Broadway guy" Ron Field's dance style was totally foreign to me. I was intimidated just to be there, but with this unusual style facing me, I was outright scared.

So, there I was—on the one hand very nervous, and on the other I was hanging onto the knowledge that I somehow possessed this superior training. On still another hand, I was totally new at this commercial audition stuff, and on even another hand (I know, way too many hands), the choreographer was bound to be impressed with my vibrant performance skills . . . wasn't he? Well, since I had already run out of hands, I took a deep breath and put on my best "look out baby here I come" attitude and pro-ceeded.

As we broke up into groups to do the dance, I was able to size up the comp-etition. To my relief, watching each group that preceded me left me more and more confident. (Pretty cocky, wasn't I?) My thoughts went something like this: "Who's that clown, he can't even do a decent pirouette, wait till Mr. Field sees my four or five turns. That guy's as exciting as my grandmother knitting her winter shawl, wait till Ron (I was starting to feel closer to the man) sees me hit those accents. Ha, that guy belongs in the old folks home, he's got to be at least 30! Boy, will Ronny (he's my buddy now) be impressed when he sees me take the floor".

In reality, there were plenty of really good dancers there. There were seasoned professionals I eventually had the good fortune of knowing, working with and learning from. But still, on another one of my many hands, I could see there were also some who probably shouldn't have been there. Funny how, at the time, I seemed to notice only them.

My turn finally came. After one time through, I felt pretty good. We were asked to go again. Okay, one more time. I can do it. I'm ready, I'm pumped, and I am totally psyched. Then I saw "Broadway Guy" Ron looking my way. That's gotta be good, right? The music started, the assistant counted us in and we were off. I put everything I had into it. He was looking at me so this was my chance—go Dennon, GO!

I used everything I ever learned and began hitting those accents like I was knocking balls out of the park. I was explosive, sharp, wispy and cutting, if I do say so myself (and believe me I was probably the only one who would). I had created a combination of an exploding firework spectacular with a tsunami chaser kicking up everything in my pathway. Whew, when I finished, I was totally spent. I had nothing left. No way could I do any better than that.

At that moment I saw the "Broadway Guy" walking toward me. Okay, okay, I thought, be calm, be cool, pretend not to notice. I wasn't exactly cool—more like the deer caught by headlights standing frozen in the middle of the road. He came right up to me, face to face, nose to nose. "Be cool", I again told myself. I assumed he'd probably compliment me on my insightful interpretation of his choreography. Or he'd ask my name in order to remember me for later. He started to speak . . . here it comes. He pointed to his assistant, looked completely annoyed at me and said, "Now do it like that!", and then walked away.

Huh? What'd he say? Is that it? Do it like that? Ugh! Where was the "Great job kid!" or "Where have you been all these years?" Good golly Miss Molly, my first commercial audition and the choreographer's response to my best, gut-wrenching effort was "NOW DO IT LIKE THAT!"

I was no longer the deer standing frozen in the middle of the road. I was the victim of a drive-by hit-and-run from my good buddy, "Broadway Guy" Ron Field. I had been sideswiped right in the middle of my overly inflated ego, and cruelly reduced to nothing more than road kill.

Now, the purpose of my recounting this most inauspicious beginning to a professional career that has spanned some 40-plus years is to get to that simple piercing moment that cut so deep, yet proved to be so profound, that it continually resonates in my brain, like the bells of Notre Dame at the hands of Quasimodo, every dancing day of my life.

To set the record straight, I did get the job. It was the first of many times I worked for Ron Field, and that day began the process of my understanding the monumental importance and implications of what he said. Throughout my performing career, as I worked for different choreographers and directors (all with their own distinct styles, techniques, methods, personalities and peculiarities), what became clearer and clearer to me was something I had never heard mentioned in any of my classes. It's a principle that sounds simple on the surface, but is oh so very important.

It is simply not enough to be a well-trained, technically proficient dancer. It doesn't matter how many pirouettes you can do or how high you can jump. What???? **In the professional world, if you don't understand, assimilate and digest the particular technique and style of the choreographer, and perform the steps or combinations in the way that he or she intends . . . you are essentially useless.**

If I was going to be a successful working dancer, I needed to "smarten up." My job was not (listen close, for this is a mighty big WAS NOT) just to show off what I believed were my superior skills while doing my own personal interpretation of the given combination, thereby ignoring the intent of the choreographer. Conversely, my job was (listen again, this is an even bigger WAS) to take the training, skills and talent I've worked so hard to cultivate over the years and serve (you heard me correctly, I said SERVE) the choreographer's desires for his or her piece.

Let me state it this way: I needed to understand the choreographer's concept, ideas and objectives (not mine), for a given piece and do my very best to utilize his or her style (not mine) to bring it to fruition. As I say to my more advanced classes, the dancer's job is to make the choreographer's work, work. Here's the thing . . .

THiNG # 2

iT'S NOT GOOD ENOUGH TO BE GOOD . . . YOU NEED TO BE SMART!

In the professional world, a decent, preferably good, even more preferably excellent technique is expected. The first phase of any audition is to eliminate those who really shouldn't be there. Once you've narrowed it down to those who possess a decent, workable technique, you then search for the smart ones.

My, how times have changed . . .

It has become increasingly clear to me that over the past few decades there has been a significant change in how students understand and approach their learning/work. In my day, it was demanded that we put 100% effort into everything we did, or we risked being ridiculed, mocked, and totally embarrassed. These days, mocking is frowned upon, but when I was young, the very risk of being singled out kept us on our toes—something incredibly important to us dancer-type people.

There's an old saying, or the first part of an old saying, that old geezers like me simply cannot resist using. I just used it—maybe you picked up on it. It's generally met with a "here he goes again" groan, but when you reach a certain age, its use somehow seems mandatory. It starts out, "In my day", or "When I was your age", then continues on to point out how much tougher the old geezer had it when he was coming up. As a young person I never thought I'd succumb to such stereotypical oration, but alas, I'm as guilty as anyone, except, I've personalized it a bit. When it becomes necessary to excoriate my students for not working to their potential, I'll intensify my demeanor and blurt out in my very best Mr. Potter's voice: **"When I was your age . . . I was much younger!" (Dennonism #1)**

My left turn on the second half of this time-honored saying generally gets a laugh, but there's also something deeper I'm getting at. Underneath the obvious silliness is an admission that I, just like they, started out as a raw, befuddled novice searching for knowledge, direction, and a dance belt that would not crimp my style! Though I never was able to do much about that third thing, I am able to offer direction and, hopefully, with the help of this book, pass on some of the wonderful knowledge and insights I've acquired over decades of "real-world" experience.

An eternal pas de deux . . .

My partner in life, dance, and every other way, is someone for whom I have the greatest amount of love, admiration, and respect. Sayhber (pronounced saber—like the sword) was already an accomplished dancer when I met her. She had appeared on the cover of Dance Magazine at age 19, and was making her mark in the L.A. dance scene. We met when I joined the Steven Peck Jazz Company, where I was able to learn a great deal about dancing, music, and training just by watching her. Anyway, to this point as I write, she and I have been working professionals for over 40 years. Together that makes over 80 years of practical, in-the-trenches, training, performing, choreographing and teaching experience.

After all those years of teaching technique classes in Jazz, Ballet, Tap, Musical Theater, Ballroom and Latin, to all levels and all ages, we just could not stand it any longer! You'd think a teacher's job would be relatively easy. You explain and demonstrate how the various positions and steps are to be executed, and then the eager students would dive in, and bingo, they're dancing. Well, not so fast. It became increasingly evident to us that before the process I described could work, we first had to teach students a very important lesson. Something many seem to have little or no clue about. Ready? The lesson was in how to take class. You heard me, I said "how." Believe me, most students, even those who've been dancing for years, do not fully understand how much their success is dependent on them.

That brings me to the title of this book, *On The Floor*. You've heard the expression "putting yourself on the line". Putting yourself on the line is what you do when you deem yourself ready. The line is a place to be judged in order to see what you already know, or can do, such as a job interview, or as it was for me, the audition for the Oscars. It's often an emotionally draining experience because somebody else is determining whether you're right for a possible position and that means possible rejection. This moment is beautifully conveyed in the Broadway Show, *A Chorus Line*, where anxious dancers literally place themselves on a line and sing the song "I Hope I Get It", which contain the immortal lyrics, "Please God, I need this job!"

There is no way to completely alleviate one's nerves in such a situation, but there is a way to maximize one's chances of being selected. Open your eyes really wide now, for what I'm about to say is vitally important. Before you can put yourself on a line, with any real chance of success, you first need to get on the floor! The floor is the classroom, the studio, the sports field—basically, any place you go to prepare yourself for your future success. The floor is the workplace, whatever, and wherever that may be.

That brings us to the "this" in the sub-title, *"If You Don't Love This, You Just Plain Don't Love Dancing"!* "This" refers to any part of the training/work process in any part of the class, rehearsal or practice phase. It's about understanding the ever-important systematic series of actions that are necessary to do in order to learn, grow or achieve. In other words, it's about overcoming our own lazy tendencies in order to do what that great overachiever from the 1970s sit-com, George Jefferson, did—move on up. (By the way, Sayhber and I appeared on a *Jefferson's* episode entitled, "Every Night Fever".)

Both the title and subtitle of this book (thesis really) can be taken literally for those of us who dance, or metaphorically for anyone wishing to achieve greatness.

A book in three acts . . .

Keeping in the spirit of the theater, I've divided this book into three acts. Act One is called "Steppin' In It . . . Big Time!", the meaning of which will reveal itself as you read. My aim is to demystify this enigmatic thing we call art, as well as the most peculiar of persons—the artist. I've no doubt put myself in harm's way by listing what I believe to be the necessary components that one must possess in order to deserve the title of "artist". (Did I say deserve?) I then narrow the scope to the crazy, wackadoo-dle world of dance, and that even stranger creature, the dancer.

Act Two, entitled "It's Your Mess!", zeros in on the concepts of excellence and success. It is devoted to anyone who truly desires a breakthrough in his or her learn-ing, growth, and achievement. You'll discover the four factors that determine a person's success, including the one factor that is most dependent on you. We also reveal the results of an exploratory surgery we performed on the rarest of individuals we call *those precious, exceptional, excellent few*, revealing ten keys that lead to ultimate success. Act Two concludes with a chapter on what I believe to be the most important, as well as the most neglected, principle, or "key". . . one you're not going to want to miss.

Act Three, "Clearing The Air!", is directed toward anyone who sits, stands or dances in a position of authority. To put it bluntly, we're talking about leadership. The chapter deals with what those in charge can do in order to better create a work environ-ment that maximizes productivity. Warning! Some may very well take offense as I make what I believe to be a clear distinction between your average everyday instructor and the much more extraordinary, much more effective "educator".

Here's the "THING". . .

As you've experienced already, I highlight what I believe to be important teaching principles I call **"Things"**. You've read two already, and there are many more throughout the book. Also included are many of my own sayings, come to be known as **"Dennonisms"**. Most of my students, past and present, are familiar with them, but here they are presented with a more complete explanation. Also look for **"Steven's Sayings"**. These are a few of the insightful, provocative, and ofttimes politically incorrect sayings uttered by our beloved mentor, Mr. Steven Peck. You'll hear more about him as we go along.

Though I'm doing the actual writing here, please know that everything you read reflects both Sayhber's and my thoughts, beliefs and conclusions. Basically, that means don't just blame me for what you read. Whatever assertion, or argument I make, consider it having come from the two of us. For convenience, I may mostly use "I", but remember it's really "we".

Whether or not you're involved in dance, or any of the arts, or just wish to improve your situation, you're going to find this book helpful. The concepts and prin-ciples contained herein transcend any particular subject area. They can be applied to any workplace environment, be it artistic, athletic, or academic. That's my belief and I'm sticking to it, but you be the judge . . . or you could go have a pizza, it's your call.

So here it is, my book, my argument, theory, notion (thesis really) -- gathered from 80 plus years of on-the-job training by two people who absolutely adore the art and science of dance -- about the arts, dance, and on how to better the teaching/learning, teacher/student process. As you read, I hope you'll be inspired to get "ON THE FLOOR", and remember . . . **IF YOU DON'T LOVE THIS . . . YOU JUST PLAIN DON'T LOVE DANCING!**

ACT ONE

Steppin' In It . . . Big Time!
- All Things Art -

ACT
ONE

Baryshnikov On Broadway 1980 TV Special - Rehearsal Photos: Martha Swope
Top Photo: Baryshnikov & Dennon
Bottom Photo: L-R: Don Correia, Gary Morgan, Baryshnikov, Dennon, Sammy Williams

CHAPTER ONE

WHAT IS ART AND WHO ARE ARTISTS?
DISSECTING A VERY STRANGE BREED!

"If my grandmother can do it, and she's been dead for 40 years, then how good can it be?" In 1982, for an upcoming television special, *Baryshnikov In Hollywood*, I found myself teaching both Mikhail Baryshnikov and Bernadette Peters a tango that paid homage to silent film star Rudolph Valentino. This was the second Special I did with Baryshnikov, the first being *Baryshnikov On Broadway* which we did a year earlier for choreographer Ron Field. For those of you who may not know, Baryshnikov, a Russian defector to Canada in 1974, was considered by many at the time to be the world's premiere Ballet dancer. His amazing technical skills, along with his exceptional artistry, were brilliantly showcased in the 1979 film, *Turning Point*—a film worthy of any aspiring dancer, Ballet or otherwise, to see. A two-time Tony award-winner, Peters was, and still is, one of Broadway's greatest performers. Five-time Tony award-winner, Michael Kidd, an internationally acclaimed artist in his own right, supplied the concept and the choreography. Kidd was noted for his brilliant work in such films as *Seven Brides for Seven Brothers*, *Guys and Dolls,* and *Hello Dolly*, just to name a few.

I, along with co-assistant Bonnie Evans (a Jack Cole alumni), had been right there from the start, working with Kidd on the creation of all the dance numbers. Among many other adventures we had, we spent weeks on the back lot of Universal Studios, working out the logistics of one of the big numbers that eventually made its way through the creative process.

What a great opportunity it was for me to see first-hand how Michael Kidd's amazing creative artistry would often begin with a simple clever idea, or even a simple probing question. One day, I came in to rehearsal and was met with, "Dennon, how does a duck walk?" Hmm . . . how does a duck walk, I wondered? He liked to ask questions like that. I thought for a moment, and then suggested something. Nope, it wasn't right for him. Then, he moved out on to the floor and showed Bonnie and me. There it was, a perfect duck walk! And why did he need a duck walk? Simple - before he could stage the Hans Christian Anderson Song, "Ugly Duckling", he needed a "hook". He needed a concept from which all movements would evolve.

From that simple question which, for him, begged to be answered, he went on to stage a thoroughly charming song and dance. Unlike some choreographers I can think of, Michael Kidd was never one for just making up steps. He had to have a reason to proceed—a seed, if you will, that would germinate and grow. Just watch any of his films and you'll see how the storyline of a given scene seamlessly flows into one of the show's songs, which in turn flows ever so beautifully into one of his spectacular production numbers. You'll see how every single movement he's created is not only relevant to the song but also the show's overall storyline. There are no meaningless, superfluous steps in a Michael Kidd production. That summer was such an incredible learning experience for me, just being around one of Musical Theater's great icons—a true artist.

A true artist . . .

To the average person out there, someone who indulges in a lifelong pursuit of artistic ventures seems a pretty odd nut. They're unconventional, non-conformists, who are often misunderstood and, at times, even shunned. What kind of crazy person would choose such a life? Now don't start feeling bad for the poor artist. Many artists enjoy not being understood. That way, they retain a certain magical, mystical, almost supernatural aura, thereby validating every lofty thing they ever thought about themselves.

What about art—what exactly is that? What makes something a work of art and something else not—or is everything to be considered art? Is it art because someone likes it and not if they don't? Who gets to decide?

Let's start our exploration into the world of art by first addressing the inevitable question of subjectivity. Here's the thing . . .

THiNG # 3

ART iS SUBJECTiVE . . . AT LEAST, THAT'S MY OPiNiON!

It's actually more precise to say the interpretation, appreciation, and understanding of art is subjective. In other words, to the extent that a given work of art is liked or appreciated is totally up to the viewer. One person's insightful, thought-provoking presentation can be another's complete waste of time.

Okay, if the understanding and appreciation of art is subjective, then obviously there can be no mutually agreed-upon definition. If there is no consensus as to the meaning of the term, then art is what you, I, he, she, it believes it to be, and therefore, because there is no criteria for anyone to use, there is no purpose in trying to figure it out, right?

The Wayback Machine . . .

Let's enlist the help of Mr. Peabody and jump in the *Wayback Machine* to visit our own dear childhood. Let's set the time for age 5. There we are, sitting at a small table all decked out with lots of nifty art-making stuff. We're given the assignment to create something, anything at all, using our own imaginations and the tools at hand. I wasn't exactly sure my imagination was up to the task, but we had time before recess, so why not? At the prompting of our teacher, we commenced to drawing, coloring, cutting, pasting, glittering and otherwise making a big, big mess of things . . . and us.

Putting our mess aside, the question becomes, were we creating art? This, of course, is where subjectivity comes in. Everyone is entitled to an opinion, even world-renowned, universally celebrated art critic . . . Mom, who, by the way, was convinced that what I had created was truly inspired. Was it so, because she said so? Being I was only five years old, I really didn't care. I was just happy to be finished so I could go outside and play.

It's important to note that a person's subjective opinion (redundant, I know) is based on many factors. Knowledge and experience in a given area are going to impact how one perceives something. Someone with little or no prior experience or knowledge of classical music and/or opera may be less likely to appreciate these art forms when first exposed. If someone's only experience with dance is Hip-Hop music videos, his or her first Ballet may seem really weird. If you've never been to the theater, a dramatic play may not measure up to the excitement of such blockbuster films like *Avatar*, *Pirates of the Caribbean*, and *Harry Potter*.

My point is, though everyone is entitled to his or her opinion on any supposed work of art, his or her opinion may very well be based on outright -- don't hate me now -- ignorance. Not having any real experience with something doesn't negate one's visceral response to that something. It's just that tastes can change as a person becomes more familiar or knowledgeable in a given area. What's off-putting one day may very well be an endearing work of art the next.

To better understand what constitutes art, we need to switch our focus to the person who creates the art. Most people who dance, sing, play music, paint and the like fall into the "dabbler" category. They're a casual participant who may enjoy the arts, but for any number of reasons (time, money, responsibilities, money, other interests, money) refrain from fully taking the plunge. I'm not trying to demean the dabbler, for art exists for everyone to enjoy, whatever one's age and whatever one's level of commit-ment. My point is simple. Being a dabbler does not an artist make.

Let's take the *Wayback Machine* a little further back in history, let's say, the Renaissance Period with the likes of Michelangelo and Leonardo da Vinci. In those days becoming an artist was something only a few exceptional (some would argue peculiar) people would aspire to. A life of producing interesting, and meaningful art was oftentimes a lonely one and generally not very profitable. These artists and others spent endless hours agonizing over the outcome of their work. They were known to have rarely been satisfied with the completion, not wanting to give it up because they knew with more time they could improve upon it. Da Vinci's Mona Lisa is said to be an example of this.

By contrast, in our culture today almost anything, from an unintended scratch on the medicine cabinet mirror to Bowser's distinctively designed doo-doo mess in the backyard, is considered art and is completely finished needing no refinement after the first draft or, in the case of Bowser, first deposit. There is to be no distinction made be-tween the "serious" practitioner of the arts and the "dabbler", nor between the intended artwork or one's uncontrollable biological function.

Now it stands to reason that if Bowser can be considered an artist for doing his dastardly daily duty in the backyard, then we who poured out our heart and soul -- designing, cutting and gluing, all the while agonizing over whether we'd finish in time for recess -- also deserve the pres-tigious title "artist", right?

Here's the thing . . .

THiNG # 4

IF EVERYONE'S AN ARTiST THEN NO ONE'S AN ARTiST!

If anyone and everyone who ever produced anything is considered an artist, then no one is an artist, for the term is rendered meaningless. Names, terms are used to distinguish something or someone from something or someone else. If everyone is an artist there's no need for the term because there's nothing to distinguish.

• • DEFiNiTiON TiME • •

I've thought long and hard and have come up with what I believe to be a solid definition of what I call a "true" artist. It's another long sentence, so take a deep breath before you begin.

Artists are visionaries (first component: **Vision**) with some inexplicable need and drive to create something stemming from a strong point of view (second component: **Point of View**) that is uniquely their own, utilizing well-developed skills (third component: **Well-Developed Skills**) with a variety of tools and instruments, and are fully committed and compelled to spend vast amounts of time (fourth component: **Commitment/Sacrifice**), maybe even a lifetime, forsaking more profitable ventures, continually creating pieces (fifth component: **Productivity**) while endeavoring to fill a need that they themselves may not fully understand.

Stop! . . . Don't move and read that again; I'll wait.

I hear you: "Who does this guy think he is . . . how dare he"? Well, I am me, the one articulating this theory, and remember, I make a clear distinction between a serious practitioner of the arts and the dabbler. I concede that what someone produces at any given time can be considered a work of art by the person doing the work and the beholder, but does that person really deserve the title of artist?

It is my contention that a person (not Bowser, or some monkey at the zoo) needs all five of the five essential components before he or she can be, or should be, considered an artist. You see, I believe the designation or title, if you will, of "artist" should be a prized one that is not easily or lightheartedly bestowed . . . certainly not on one whom only dabbles.

Let's break down each of the five components and see how they work. Here they are once again:

1. Vision   2. Point of View   3. Well-Developed Skills
4. Commitment/Sacrifice   5. Productivity

Component # 1: VISION

It's clear to me that the artist has somewhat heightened, keenly-developed senses. His or her imagination can soar as he or she sees something in the sky that no one else does. The artist keenly observes extraordinary subtleties and nuances in human behavior. He or she becomes almost aroused by the sweet fragrance of a blossoming flower. There is something in the sound and feeling of the wind that awakens the artist, and there is something in the stillness and absolute dead silence that mesmerizes.

Simply put, the artist's physical and emotional sensibilities seem to be heightened, ever-present, and ever-willing to embrace the moment. They seemed to be blessed (some might say cursed) with a deeper, more profound perception of things.

With that in mind, it is not hard to understand how an artist can be inspired and impassioned beyond the "norm" (another subjective term artists hate) by some or all that can be seen, heard, felt, smelled, or tasted. That inspiration and passion then drives the imagination to envision things "mere mortals" do not. Those "things" eventually end up on the canvas, the page, or in a song, play or dance. Component # 1: VISION.

Component # 2: POINT OF VIEW

Every human being shares commonalities with every other human being, yet at the same time every human has a uniqueness to them. We all have fingers, yet our fingerprints are one-of-a-kind. The same is true of our individual perspective. How we see things, perceive things, understand things, and appreciate things are distinctly our own, i.e. subjective. We all see the clouds in the sky, but we are not all affected in the same way by those clouds. Ten different painters can paint the same landscape and skyline from the same place and come up with markedly different finished works. Ten ballerinas can perform the same role on stage and each one (if she's a real artist and not just a technician) will bring something new, fresh, and clearly distinctive to the role.

Why? Because no two people are born with the exact same talents, having had the exact same training, having been influenced by the exact same people, having lived through the exact same circumstances, in the exact same geographical location. In other words, as much as we all have in common, we are each a unique creation of Almighty God.

Therefore, a true artist's original work, is not a paint-by-numbers copy of someone else's previous vision-version. If one painter's version of the ocean is exactly like another's, why bother? If one dancer's version of *Giselle* is exactly like another's, what's the point (of view)? Imitation may be the greatest form of flattery, but it also reveals the limitations of the person's work.

I have found over and over again that there are many in the art world who suffer from the delusion that they are creating something new when they really are not. They are simply re-creating, or more precisely, imitating. They may be excellent mimics, possessing excellent technique (that's the craft part), yet still only producing imitations, so they are not, in my opinion, real artists producing real art.

Why? They are missing the first two components. They are reproducing someone else's vision (not theirs) of something that was generated from someone else's point of view (not theirs). Artists don't imitate, they originate. Here's the thing . . .

THING # 5

REAL ARTISTS EXPOSE THEMSELVES!

Every artist's (every person's) unique personal perspective is informed and dictated by their own life history. That includes family, friends, education, economic situation, etc., etc. Each artist brings his or her own "fingerprint" perspective (distinct point of view) to his or her work. It is that viewpoint of a given idea, situation or thing that gets revealed or *exposed* and, hopefully, discovered in their work.

Some artists quite intentionally, while making no apologies about it, use their art to editorialize or comment on something. Others are much more subtle and nuanced. There are some who are downright devious in revealing their views to the point of it being subliminal. Then there are those who aren't even aware of the extent to which they do it. This kind of artist works more on instinct and intuition and may even deny their work says anything at all. Actually by denying that their work says or reveals anything says a lot about the artist and their art right there.

Beyond the esthetic aspect, the deeper task of the viewer of any given artwork or presentation is to search for the artist's reason for creating it. Somewhere in an artist's work you will gain insight into his or her views on politics, social issues, life, death, faith, love, family, relationships, or anything and everything including art itself.

As I said, it can be quite overt or very, very subtle, but if it is real art by a real "artist", it'll be there, somewhere. Component # 2: POINT OF VIEW.

Component # 3: WELL-DEVELOPED SKILLS

Here's where the craft comes in and the doggy goes out. (Remember Bowser's "still life" doo-doo rendition in the backyard where he is no doubt editorializing on the meaning of life!) First off, you must know there is a big distinction to be made between "training" and "talent". I won't be commenting on one's talent now . . . we'll get to that in Chapter Five.

Whether it (whatever the "it" one does) comes easily or with some degree of difficulty, every artist must develop and continually refine their skills. Dedicated musicians will practice several hours per day for their entire career developing, perfecting and maintaining their skills. Serious actors will return to class or rehearsal to work scenes over and over again, digging deeper and deeper, searching for the truest, clearest meaning behind their character's behaviors. Painters will paint canvas after canvas trying to better convey what's in their mind's eye.

Committed dancers (make your own joke here) continually return to class, day after agonizing day, doing the same intensely difficult exercises literally tens of thousands of times all for the purpose of making what they do look beautiful and effortless. Truth be told, without well-developed skills, it's impossible to bring one's vision to life. Component # 3: WELL-DEVELOPED SKILLS.

Component # 4: COMMITMENT/SACRIFICE

As I mentioned before, to the sensible, dare I say "normal" person, the artist seems to be a particularly odd nut. After all, what kind of person spends hours and hours doing something that no one really asked for, and for which there is no guarantee of any acceptance, let alone remittance, all the while forsaking other more profitable endeavors?

As a matter of fact, for many young (and not so young) aspiring artists, there is a need to work various side jobs in order to earn the necessary funds to pay for lessons and practice time to acquire and develop the requisite skills to do the art they so desperately want to do in the first place. In other words, obtaining and maintaining the necessary skills to create their art means spending money, not earning it. How dopey is that?

In addition to sacrificing more lucrative ventures, becoming an artist requires sacrificing his or her social life as well. I know it did for me. While my peers were going to school football games and dances, or just hanging out together, I was attending dance, voice and acting classes. That's what artists do – they make a strong commitment and then sacrifice! Component # 4: COMMITMENT/SACRIFICE.

Component # 5: PRODUCTIVITY

Artists have this insatiable need to create. Yes, it's a need. Creativity is at the very core of every artist's being. Often the artist him or herself knows not why; they simply must create and continually create their art.

My theory is it has to do with the first two components. Their heightened senses act as springboards for blossoming ideas (vision) that continually present themselves, without any prompting whatsoever, at which point he or she feels compelled to express him or herself as only he or she can (point of view). Whether they believe what they've created is a genuine masterpiece or not doesn't really matter. What's important to the artist is to continually produce.

Though it sounds odd, the artist understands that the answer to the questions and problems that arise in any given work lies in the next work. That is to say, with each successive endeavor, the artist works to improve upon any previous venture.

The choreographer wants to better connect the movement with the music. The composer wants his or her next love song to be the one that more readily melts the hearts of all who hear it. The lyricist endeavors to be more stylish and wittier in his or her lyrics. The painter searches for better ways to portray emotions, so he or she eagerly begins the next project to hopefully discover how.

14

With few exceptions, it's only through creating piece after piece that the artist improves and refines his or her technique, style, and talents. It is primarily through choreographing dance after dance, writing song after song, painting canvas after canvas that one develops his or her skills, matures in his or her ability to express him or herself, and really finds his or her unique "voice". Component # 5: PRODUCTIVITY.

There you have it, the five essential components I believe a person must have in order to deserve the title artist. Once again, they are:

1. Vision   2. Point of View   3. Well-Developed Skills
4. Commitment/Sacrifice   5. Productivity

What's important to understand is that the artist does not approach what they do as merely a job. It's definitely work, often hard work, but their work is not work in the conventional sense of the word—it's a calling. By that I mean it's something they can't ignore or escape, for it's ever present in their hearts and minds.

Day or night, without warning it can pull the artist's attention away from whatever else they may be doing. The artist doesn't clock in at a certain time in order to perform designated duties that all too often become routine and boring. To further understand art, we must now pivot on over to art's necessary companion.

The art of craft . . .

The craftsperson is someone whom the artist often needs in order to bring his or her art to fruition. The architectural designer needs construction workers, the auto designer needs assembly workers, the costume designer needs seamstresses, the choreographer needs dancers, the songwriter needs singers, and the list goes on and on.

The question becomes: Is a craftsperson also an artist? The answer is maybe. It all depends on how he or she approaches his or her work. I've seen technicians on theater and film sets who essentially do what is asked for and nothing more. They hammer nails, paint sets, repair costumes, dress sets, etc., all with little enthusiasm. In other words, what they do provides a paycheck and that's all that matters to them.

The word I would attribute to the non-artist craftsperson is "technician". Some may be good or even excellent at what they do, but their work is emotionless, passionless, and detached . . . certainly not artistic. This is not a criticism, but a description.

The dancer is the perfect example of someone who should strive to be both an excellent craftsperson (technician) as well as artist. Unfortunately, there are many professional dancers whose technique is excellent, yet their work lacks passion, with little or no interpretation or personal style.

The primary indicator that a craftsperson is neither an artist, nor wishes to be one, is that they are easily satisfied with their work and see no need to put forth more time and effort than is minimally required in order to complete their assigned task. In other words, their work (again no criticism) is a just a job.

On the other hand, the craftsperson/artist does not see his or her work as just a "job", but more as an opportunity to explore, investigate, and discover new possibilities in a collaborative way with the original visionary/creative artist.

Like any artist, they become completely engrossed in the work as if the original vision was theirs, knowing the final outcome will reflect their artistry as well. He or she is often not fully satisfied with their completed work and are in need of no external prodding to spend whatever time is necessary to do the best work possible.

This is not to say that they would do their assignment without compensation; it's just that after the "deal" is made, they do their work with little or no thought of the financial aspect. That's why they are sought after. They are hired because it isn't just a job to them, and their input and contribution so adds to the final product/fully realized piece that the end result is often better than the original creator/designer imagined.

Whether one is a creative artist or a craftsperson/artist, they both have the same intense drive to continually develop their skills. Why? The answer takes us back to the five components. Get ready for another one of my long sentences so, once again, take a deep breath before you begin.

Because the artist has this mental picture/image of something **(Vision)**, along with how that something ought (not could, but ought) to be portrayed or conveyed **(Point of View)**, which gives him or her this extraordinary, almost unexplainable (though I'm doing my best), urge, drive and compulsion **(Commitment/Sacrifice)** to make it ("it" being the vision) happen, it becomes absolutely necessary (not optional) to continually work at developing his or her craft **(Well-Developed Skills)** so that the artist's vision can become better, more fully portrayed, performed and/or realized **(Productivity)**.

Each art form has certain things in common with the others and many things specific to itself. One thing for certain they have in common is that they each require an enormous amount of time and effort to develop the requisite skills (craft) to be good at it. Countless hours upon days upon weeks upon months upon years upon decades are needed for the development of one's skills to better and more fully realize one's vision and express one's point of view.

Please know I don't want to scare anyone away from delving into the arts to begin expressing him or herself before he or she has what can be considered "fully" developed skills. It's just that the someone who fancies him or herself a true artist will be the someone who is drawn into a lifelong pursuit of developing, refining, and otherwise honing their skills so they can make the art they so passionately desire to do.

Conclusion:

I know I'm holding extremely high standards for one to qualify as an artist, but I believe the title of "artist" should be earned over time, because its value, like that of diamonds and gold, is derived from its rarity, as well as the hard work that's necessary to achieve it.

I'm not saying that if you do not possess all the components I've described above then you cannot or should not involve yourself in the arts. Not at all, the arts are there for everyone to enjoy to the extent they wish. There is an enormous amount of joy to be gained from participating in some form of music, dance, painting, etc., regardless of one's ultimate objective. One need not be an aspiring professional in order to participate. I encourage everyone to participate, by all means, dabble away. What I am saying is unless you have all the components, you are probably not what I call a "true artist", meaning a serious practitioner. You may love dancing, singing, or painting, but being an artist requires a real commitment, not just a part-time effort.

Having said that, one must concede that a dabbler may very well create something that someone, or many someones, may deem an actual work of art. We cannot discount subjectivity. Though it pains me to say it, for some, even what Bowser did, intentionally or not, in the backyard could be thought of as a work of art. That doesn't mean that Bowser deserves to be called an artist, though. It's just that there's no accounting for personal taste . . . or smell.

If someone is into the avant-garde, the peculiar and the irregular, and they find such things aesthetically pleasing, aromatically arousing, and it speaks to them (emotionally and intellectually), then for that person (though I'd hate to be the one to put a frame around it) it may be considered art.

I, however, still would not yet bestow the title of "artist" on the dabbler (which includes Bowser). He's a part-time practitioner who was able to create something that somebody else actually liked.

He had what could be called a momentary or singular inspiration (Vision) with a particular perspective (Point of View) with enough proficiency (Well-Developed Skill) and spent just enough time (Commitment) to make the one work of art. So, why in the world should he not be called an artist?

Here's the thing . . .

THING # 6

ARTISTS ARE EXTREMELY FERTILE CREATURES!

Artists do not produce one "something"—they produce many "somethings" day after day, week after week, month after month, year after year, and decade after decade. Their personality make-up is one of needing to continually express themselves through their art. In other words, Component # 5: Productivity.

Now, if a person begins committing more time to creating more work and develops a portfolio that demonstrates an ongoing commitment that goes beyond a singular inspiration, then he or she may very well deserve the title "artist". Exactly how much work? It's not about any particular quantity. It's about the continuous ongoing creation of whatever the art is. I just believe that one must earn the title of "artist" over time by demonstrating their commitment and "creative fruitful fertility".

Warning! - Gratuitous nudity ahead!

Proceed if you dare as I reveal that, as far as I'm concerned, the Emperor is completely, totally, stripped down butt-naked!

There is a certain kind of "art" out there that can only be described as cheap, easy and sensationalistic! Cheap art exists (so it seems to me) to invoke a response, usually emotional discomfort, embarrassment and even anger, by simply disrespecting sacred conventions under the guise of "pushing the envelope". The person who makes such art is uninterested in developing his or her skills in order to better realize a vision. Why do I say this? Because it takes no real skill or talent to produce this stuff. To me it's another case of the Emperor's New Clothes—nothing really there, but those who don't wish to be ostracized from the elitist "in crowd" often buy into it.

I'm not talking about what may be classified as "lowbrow" or "pop surrealism" where the art is centered on pop culture. I am talking about taking human or animal waste and throwing it at a canvas, placing a frame around it and hanging it in a gallery. Or, taking a jar of one's own urine and placing a crucifix supporting the body of Christ in it. Then there's a guy who hangs upside down on a rope naked with his head covered in plastic wrap and a carrot sticking out of his . . . well you get the picture.

Here's my question: How many years did the so-called artist work to develop the skills to throw dung on a canvas? How bright, clever, and witty is the guy who, just because he could, offend an entire community of religious believers? How about the naked guy hanging from a rope . . . what'd he do to prepare himself, besides shop for produce? This stuff is sensationalistic to be sure, sometimes entertaining, and always weird, but art? For me it is just an easy, cheap way to evoke a response without utilizing real talent or developed skills for the purposes of getting attention, which seems to be their only real desire.

Please understand, religion or sexuality or any subject should not be off limits to artists. Some of the greatest works of art celebrate, question, and even criticize these themes. It's just that there is real talent mixed with excellence of craft in these works of art. Art should evoke all kinds of emotions, but if the only point of a piece is to offend in order to gain notoriety, then one need never study, work hard or agonize over their finished work.

My defense of what I believe to be real art or "true" artists is no different than any other profession's defense of who should be thought of as a "true" professional in their respective field. I simply have the belief that the designation, or "title" of artist should be reserved for those who deserve it by virtue of the fact they've earned it. After all, we don't call anyone who ever applied a bandage to someone a doctor, or anyone who ever testified in a courtroom a lawyer, or anyone who's ever changed a spark plug a mechanic. "Titles" are bestowed on those who deserve it because they've earned it.

In the area of dance, here's one way I determine if the performance was worth my time and money: **"If my grandmother can do it, and she's been dead for 40 years, then how good can it be?" (Dennonism #2)** If anyone who's never taken a dance class could come in off the street and do it, then why would I want to see it? This is what I see at a lot of college performances—a whole bunch of people running around the stage making agonizing sounds and shapes. At today's prices, if I'm going to buy a ticket to see something, I want to see something that only a select few can do which demonstrates the artist's passion, determination, craft, talent and . . . life-long commitment!

In defense of pointy pirate hats . . .

I'm not here to say that artists are better than anyone else, or that they should be put up on a pedestal to be idolized. No way. Many artists are eccentric, lonely, and live outside of convention. They're known for cutting off ears, abusing drugs, rarely sleeping, and walking around completely naked wearing pointy pirate hats (but enough about me).

It's also true that in many everyday situations they can be quite inept. They spend so much time working on their art that they often have little time to cultivate other important aspects of life, like relationships, fixing leaking faucets, and dressing oneself (stop, enough about me).

The world needs artists, but it also needs farmers, doctors, lawyers, accountants, firefighters, police officers, gardeners, and even (heaven help us), politicians. All are valuable and contribute to the world's needs. By the way, there is artistry connected with all those professions, but that's a whole other book.

So, once again I ask you . . . is anyone who spends a lifetime in pursuit of creating things that nobody asked for in the first place, really sane? Maybe, maybe not, but for those of us who do, ah . . . there's that elusive prize of the occasional moment of indescribable ecstasy of having experienced a truly creative moment, or of having completed a truly creative endeavor that all artists seek—that's what we're attracted, dare I say addicted, to!

Baryshnikov In Hollywood 1982 TV Special – On the set photos: Private
Top Photo: Dennon, Baryshnikov, Jerry Evans
Bottom Photo: Choreographer Michael Kidd between takes

The Ann-Margret Show 1977 Las Vegas Hilton Hotel - Photo: James Joseph
Dennon with Ann-Margret

CHAPTER TWO
FROM ARTIST TO AUDIENCE - THE ROAD TRAVELED
IT TAKES THREE TO TANGO!

"Remembering the steps is the least you can do!" In the late 1970s, Sayhber and I choreographed a nine-minute production number for Ann-Margret's nightclub show. I had been dancing with Ann-Margret for a couple of years, touring the country, when I was asked if I'd like to choreograph something for her. Would I??? This kind of offer doesn't come along all that often, so I immediately contacted Sayhber and told her about it. The very next day Sayhber was on a plane flying to Vegas, where the A-M show was performing, and joined me at Caesar's Palace.

We worked all day long on an idea we pitched to both Ann-Margret and her manager/husband, Roger Smith, after the show that night. They were quite surprised we had something to show on such short notice. Well, I wasn't going to let this opportunity slip by. We had an idea for a Latin production number that we mapped out on paper, as well as having gathered together some of the music we might use. We showed them the partnership section that I would be doing with her. She seemed to like what she saw and had us teach her a bit of it. I think what she liked most was the fact that I could partner her in such a way that she felt very secure. (Partnership is something both Sayhber and I have always been noted for.) I could put her in a lift and keep her there—pretty important for such a big star. Anyway, that began the beginning of a creative process that took several weeks to complete.

In this chapter I want to explore the three-step procedure that makes up the artistic process. If you're an experienced artist, you're no doubt familiar with each of the steps. If you're just starting out, or you're an interested patron of the arts, it'll be good for you to understand the roadway that all art must travel. Here they are:

1. Creative Artist   2. Performing/Interpretive Artist   3. Audience/Recipient of Art

Step # 1: CREATIVE ARTIST
The creative artist is the originator of any given work of art. He or she begins with a single inspired idea. It's the vision we spoke about in the previous chapter. The painter, for example, will stand in front of a completely blank canvas, staring out at the horizon. As inspiration comes, he or she begins expressing on canvas what that horizon is saying to him or her. The sculptor starts with some kind of base material such as clay, stone, wood, etc., then, utilizing his or her talents, training, and inspired idea, begins molding, carving or chipping away to create something.

The writer is a classic example of creative artist. The writer literally begins with a blank sheet of paper, then digs deep into his or her own creative, hopefully fertile, imagination, spending weeks, months, and sometimes even years to bring to fruition an idea that, for him or her, just simply must be expressed.

The choreographer is another example of the creative artist. He or she creates a visual, spatial art experience from an inspired idea that for him or her also begs to be produced. Sometimes that begging comes from producers and directors who've hired the choreographer, and other times from the choreographer's own personal need to express his or her perspective (point-of-view) on something. Unlike other creative artists, the choreographer's base material consists of actual living human-type beings.

The distinction here is most creative artists work alone, using base materials that are essentially inanimate and mute. The novelist sits at the computer for hours and the computer hardly ever asks for a break. The sculptor works with clay and, if he or she feels the need, will slap that clay silly till it cooperates or throw it out and start over. You won't find too much of that happening in the dance world these days, though once upon a time, certain Hollywood and Broadway choreographers were known to get a bit "physical" with their dancers.

There are, of course, many other kinds of creative artists I'll mention briefly here. In the theater, for example, there is the director, costume designer, set designer, lighting designer, sound designer, hair designer, and make-up designer—all of whom must use their creative talents to form, fashion, and otherwise produce a very necessary element in the overall theater process. Then there are the many workers (craftspeople) who, as I mentioned in the previous chapter, may be artists in their own right. Outside the theater category, there is the architect, the landscape artist, and I'm sure others you can think of as well.

So, once again, what makes them "creative" artists? They basically start with little or nothing, except the inspired idea, and design, write, paint, or choreograph something that has either never been done before, or they take something that may have been done before, and re-create it in a brand new, "inspired" way.

Step # 2: PERFORMING/INTERPRETIVE ARTIST
Step two is essential because a given work of art remains unrealized until it is presented to the world. The performing artist, also known as an interpretive artist, is the presenter of any given artwork. He or she uses his or her talents, along with their highly trained technical abilities, to present that which was created by the creative artist.

It is important to note that the performing artist is also a creative artist. It is just for the purpose of understanding and differentiating the two that I use the terms "creative" and "performing". One originates the material and the other originates the performance. It is the performer's job to create an original performance by infusing life into the creative artist's original idea.

Think of it this way: The songwriter needs the singer, the music writer needs the musician, and the playwright needs the actor. Each performing artist brings his or her unique talents and technical abilities to the process, which results in a one-of-a-kind, completed presentation. The "one-of-a-kind" concept is very important. If the performing artist is a true artist, there will be no two exact interpretations and presentations of any character, dance, or song in the theater. There ought to be no two same, exact interpretations of Juliet, Hamlet, Stanley Kowalski, or any other character you can think of.

It's important to note that the artistry of one's performance is not the result of one's ability to remember the choreographer's steps or the playwright's words. No matter how many times one has sung a song, or recited a poem, or played a character on stage, the performer's artistry can be measured by his or her ability to present their material in a fresh, inspired way, as if they're doing so for the very first time.

Our "creative father", Steven Peck, often referred to the concept of: **"Marrying the music!". (Steven's Saying # 1)** For the dancer, that has to do with making such an intimate connection to the feel, mood, and phrasing of the music that the steps and movement patterns, no matter how many times they are performed, look as if they are being birthed anew each and every time.

One of the things I tell my classes, usually after they get that pleased look on their faces just because they didn't forget anything is: **"Remembering the steps is the least you can do!" (Dennonism #3)** It's the same in the acting field. Just as remembering the steps does not a dancer make, remembering the words does not an actor make. It's what you do with those steps and words that make for an interesting, meaningful, artistic performance.

Agony or ecstasy . . .

Understand now, there are parameters set by the playwright, director, choreographer, etc. that will guide and direct the performing artist, but there is always, or should always be, enough creative leeway for the performing artist to put his or her own signature to the piece. This is what excites and energizes the performing artist to take on the task of interpreting someone else's creation in the first place. Together the creative artist and performing artist make up two thirds of the art equation. Here's the thing . . .

THiNG # 7

THE CREATiVE ARTiST AND THE PERFORMiNG ARTiST NEED EACH OTHER!

Without the performing artist the creative artist's vision is left unrealized. Without the creative artist, the performing artist is mute, or in the case of dance, motionless. The singer needs a song to sing and the songwriter needs a singer to sing it.

For the writer, composer, and choreographer, it can be an amazing experience to see their work infused with the performer's fresh energy and insight. It can also be just plain agony to see their work interpreted in such a way as to lose or defuse their original intent but, alas, it's all part of the process.

Exceptions to the rule . . .

There are some creative art forms that require no middleman. That is, there is no need of someone to present, explain, or interpret the work. It goes from the creator to the viewer/consumer without need of presentation. This kind of art stands alone. After the painting is completed, the finished work needs no one to sing it, act it, or dance it. The only need is some kind of a venue to display the work. It could be an actual gallery, or a street fair where everyone is welcome to display their work. The point is, the work stands alone for the public to interpret and appreciate as they wish. The same can be said for the finished sculpture. Some may argue that some works of art do need explaining, but most artists are generally content to the let the viewer contemplate the meaning and ultimate value of their work.

For the great American novel, it is the reader who does the interpreting. The reader gets to conjure up his or her own visions of what the writer has written. It may or may not have anything to do with what was going on in the writer's mind when writing it, but letting one's imagination soar is part of the joy of reading.

Secondly, there are those artists who function in both categories of creator and presenter. There are musicians and singers who write and sing their own material. There are dancers who create their own dances, and actors who have been known to write their own material.

It must be said, though, that even in a one-person show, where the presenter is also the creator/writer/director, there is usually need of other artists to complete the process. There are costume designers as well as lighting and set designers. All are essential to the process of completing the art experience. Whether there are one or two or more separate people involved in the creation and presentation of a given work of art, there are still two separate parts involved—the creation aspect and the performance aspect.

Step # 3: AUDIENCE/RECIPIENT OF ART

In my opinion, the part of the equation that is too often neglected when art is being discussed is the work's final destination. Whether one realizes it or not, to fully (I said *fully*) complete the art *process* (love that word) you need a recipient—that is someone to view, or hear, or taste, or touch or even smell the art.

Here's the thing . . .

THiNG # 8

ART NEEDS TO BE CONSUMED!

If a tree in the forest, which has been carved into a beautiful work of art, is hit by lightning and falls to the ground, and no one is around to see it, hear it, taste it, touch it, or smell it, will anyone applaud? No getting around it, the creative artist and the performing artist have little reason to be, if there's no one around to appreciate it.

No matter how much pleasure and satisfaction the artist gains from just doing the work, and no matter how many times the artist claims they don't care if anyone else likes it, understands it, or appreciates it, the process (I said process) of art is not complete till the consumer comes into the picture. I'm not saying they need to be catered to, but I am saying they shouldn't be ignored.

The great filmmaker, Frank Capra (*Mr. Smith Goes to Washington, Meet John Doe,* and *It's a Wonderful Life*), whose films are celebrated for their artistry and heartfelt messages, said in an interview, which was televised on TCM, that it was important to entertain first and then throw in a message. That way, the audience will more easily accept whatever message you may be wanting to convey. It wasn't beneath the great filmmaker/artist Frank Capra to take into account the eventual consumer of his work!

The puzzle is now complete . . .

The audience/recipient is the final piece of the puzzle. They complete the art process. Once again they are:

1. Creative Artist 2. Performing/Interpretive Artist 3. Audience/Recipient of Art

Though painful at times, the audience/recipient of a given work of art can give valuable feedback to the artist so he or she can determine if what they've created has been successfully conveyed and/or understood. The artist also needs some kind of validation for having contributed something of "value" to humankind.

Validation primarily comes in the form of an entranced viewer or a mesmerized listener. The appreciation of an artist's work is, often, enough for the artist to believe he or she has made a "valued" contribution to humanity. They are then encouraged to continue on down that lonely highway they've been drawn to. I know that there are some artists who say they don't need or want to be loved. They just want to know they've "affected" someone, somehow. Whether it be positive or negative, they only care that as long as they've provoked some kind of emotional response from a viewer or listener, they're satisfied.

Though many artists deny its necessity, validation is important because artists don't produce the essential, practical things that are necessary to sustain life—or do they? Hmmm. Here's the thing . . .

THiNG # 9

ART FEEDS THE INNER PERSON—THE SOUL!

Just as food feeds the body, and books feed the intellect, art feeds the soul. The consumer of art is looking to be moved in some way. Art can be the catalyst that does just that. It can entertain, encourage and inspire us. It can reveal and celebrate the beauty in life, as well as reveal and question life's painful side.

There is more to human existence than the material. There are matters of the heart and soul. A good work of art (my opinion) invites, or even insists, the recipient dive head on into an experience where they are swept away to another time, place and dimension.

Dollars certainly make sense . . .
Though a true artist will continue on anyway, an artist needs financial support. The ultimate sign of appreciation is someone willing to buy someone's finished work, or pay a fee to observe and hear the artist's work. As we know from history, sometimes this doesn't happen till after the artist's passing. Vincent Van Gogh is a perfect example of this. Widely regarded as one of history's greatest "post-impressionist" artists, he was not very appreciated during his lifetime. He committed suicide at the age of 37. I wonder what would have happened had he been a little stronger and a lot more appreciated during his lifetime?

In the next chapter I zero in on what I believe to be the strangest of all artists. Grab your Capezios and dance on over to the next page.

Dennon & Sayhber Performing
at Orange Coast College
mid-2000s
Photo: Todd Crespi

CHAPTER THREE
WHAT IS DANCE AND WHO ARE DANCERS?
AN EVEN STRANGER BREED!

"The pain you feel is your own!" Remember the lovely, sultry Cyd Charisse? Having appeared in such films as *Singing In The Rain*, *Brigadoon*, and *The Bandwagon*, just to name a few, she was one of MGM's biggest musical stars of the 1940s and 50s. Though her early training was primarily Classical Ballet, her ability to move her body in a slithery, sexy, jazzy manner was tantalizing. She also possessed an athleticism that may not have been readily apparent due to her beauty, grace and, femininity. In the film, *It's Always Fair Weather*, in which she starred along with Gene Kelly, Dan Dailey, and choreographer Michael Kidd (in a rare acting/dancing/lip-syncing role), Cyd was featured in a powerfully executed, tour de force Jazz/Ballet number set, of all places, in a boxing gym. Though there are several terrific numbers in the film, this number alone makes the film worthwhile.

Cyd was one of very few who shared the distinction of having partnered the two greatest screen dance icons, Gene Kelly and Fred Astaire, several times over. I also had the extreme good fortune of partnering her during the summer of 1974, just after I did that first Academy Awards show. By then, she was in her early 50s and still a gorgeous beauty to behold. She and her husband, also an MGM star, singer/actor Tony Martin (what a hoot he was), toured the country doing a charming nightclub act that featured Cyd's sexy dancing.

If my memory serves me correctly, we started our tour at the historic Thunderbird Hotel in Las Vegas. The hotel is no longer there, but I can still see it in my mind's eye just as clear as ever. We then went on to perform in such cities as Hyannis Port, MA, Pittsburg, PA, Cleveland, OH, Dallas, TX, and several other cities. We then finished our summer tour back at the Thunderbird Hotel. Though I can't remember all the places we played, what I do remember is that we were either performing somewhere, or we were traveling to our next destination.

I also remember that when we were in Vegas we did two shows a night, seven nights a week -- no nights off -- for something like 56 straight performances—pretty amazing when I think of it. There were four of us guys in the act—all there to sing backup for Tony Martin, and showcase the beautiful Cyd Charisse. It was quite a summer and I learned a great deal from the experience.

By the way, this was the second time I worked for my good buddy, "Broadway Guy", Ron Field. He was brought in to stage a production number reminiscent of the old MGM musicals Cyd was noted for.

During this time I was privy to how this iconic figure approached her art and craft—how she prepared, both mentally and physically, and even emotionally. It's a difficult thing to continually perform night after night, especially for a dancer, whose performance depends so much on his or her physical capabilities.

Each night I would watch Cyd prepare. I watched the other guys prepare as well. I even watched me prepare. It was fascinating to see how five professional dancers readied themselves for the evening's performance. There was the dance warm-up ritual, the putting on make-up ritual, and the vocal warm-up ritual. Sometimes, there was the kidding around ritual, all for the purposes of easing the tension. Then, just before going on, there was the getting focused ritual. That was a time of quieting oneself in order to tune out all outside distractions so one could put their full attention into the performance.

I have to tell you that, because of the grueling schedule we had, there were times when our bodies would have rather been elsewhere. Many a time, there was at least one of us nursing some kind of ache or pain—but that's par for the course when dealing with any kind of dance performance. Regardless of how one feels, the dancer perseveres, goes on stage, and convinces everyone watching that what they are doing is about the most fun, easy, and pain-free thing a person could ever do.

The dancer . . .

As is the case for all the arts, I believe that someone who makes a lifelong commitment to the art and craft of dance hasn't just made a choice, but has also answered a calling.

To the mere mortal, dancing is nothing more than movin' and groovin' to music. Some also believe it to be just about any physical movement whatsoever, whether to music or not (this makes the Modern dancers happy). To all the liberated, unconventional free thinkers out there, life itself is dance. Yes, the day-to-day moving about, taking care of our daily business is life's luscious dance.

• • DEFINITION TIME • •

To dance is: "to move rhythmically to music". So it looks like most people's description of dance is correct; dancing is movin' and groovin' to music. No doubt about it, in the most general sense of the word, that's what it is—but is that all it is?

A brief bit of dance history . . .

It seems every culture since the beginning of time has produced some sort of physical movement expression that can be labeled dance. The people who perform these "folk" dances at social gatherings generally have little or no real training, and the music that is used is native to the given area. By its very existence, it seems that people have a need, not just a desire, to express themselves through the medium of dance.

Over time, many of these folk dances have developed and grown into beautiful artistic expressions of a group of people's beliefs, history, and desires. Some of these forms of dance have continued to develop to the point of having outgrown their original intent of being merely social, religious, and/or political, to becoming something whose purpose is one of being presented in front of a large, hopefully paying, audience as both entertainment and artistic expression.

Ballet is an example of a social/cultural dance form that originated in the French courts of the sixteenth century. It began as an upper-class social dance, with some political overtones, that was danced with and by the elites in front of royalty and, over time (much time), developed into a highly technical art form embraced by the entire world. Yes, what has become the most stringent and precise of all the theatrical dance disciplines began as a social dance.

Ballroom/Latin dance also began as social dance forms, which developed into theatrical art forms with contributors from all over the world. The Waltz from Vienna, the Tango from Argentina, the Mambo/Salsa from Cuba, the Fox Trot and Swing from America, are just a few examples. Ballroom/Latin dancing remains a social dance form for all to enjoy, but there is an ever-growing number of people all over the world dedicating countless hours of training to do things within this dance genre that social dancers never even imagined.

Jazz dance has been categorized as "urban folk dance". It was a uniquely American music form called Jazz, which developed in the African American communities in the early part of the 20th century, that gave way to many social dance forms, which in turn lead the way to many theatrical dance forms, including what we think of as Jazz dance today. The enormously popular Swing dance era of the 1930s and 40s is a result of a form of Jazz labeled Swing. Yes, Swing dancing is actually a form of Jazz dance.

Other early dances of the 1920s, such as the Black Bottom and the Charleston, all came out of the early Jazz age making them, de facto, a form of Jazz dance. It was these dances, along with the burgeoning Tap dance movement, that made their way onto the Vaudeville, Burlesque, and Broadway stages, as well as early film. These dances, which began as social dance forms in urban society soon developed into much more theatrical dance/art forms.

My intention here is not to give an exhaustive study of dance history. It is only to underscore the universality of humankind's desire and need to express itself through the medium of dance, and how those dance forms evolved into something greater than their original intent. If you're interested, there are many books, articles, and videos that can be investigated.

So what can we conclude? That dancing is, quite naturally, a natural expression of the human species. It's only natural, right? The answer is . . . it depends.

The nature of dance . . .

Periodically, when I see that my students are struggling to understand something or to develop a certain skill, I'll take the opportunity to relieve their anxiety by instructing them that: **"Dancing is not natural!" (Dennonism #4)** Their looks say it all—dancing isn't natural? I tell them I'm not talking about just movin' and groovin' to the music, which many of them do pretty well.

On a side note, one thing I've learned for sure over the years is that not everyone is born with the same natural proclivity to hearing, feeling, connecting to, and moving with music. You only have to look at a group of toddlers when music is playing to see which of them, without any prompting, begins moving in perfect harmony with the rhythm, and those who just look as if they need to be "changed".
But I digress.

I further explain to my students that the kind of dance I'm referring to when I tell my class that dancing is not "natural" is the kind they're involved in that moment, which is usually Jazz or Ballet.

Of course I'm also talking about Modern, which along with Jazz and Ballet, make up what I call the big three. Whether it be a career in a concert company, or theater, or film, or television, these three are the main disciplines one needs to be proficient in. So, what exactly is natural anyway?

Here's the thing. . .

THiNG # 10

NATURAL iS WHAT YOU DO WiTHOUT HAViNG TO TAKE LESSONS!

How natural can something be if you have to take lessons? Movin' and groovin' to music may be natural for many, but the techniques of Ballet, Modern, and Jazz (and others) are forms of dance that require years of training, hence making them learned skills or behaviors.

I know I annoy many when I definitively define anything, let alone a word like "natural". Who am I to judge what's natural? I'm really just using common sense. Isn't eating natural? After all, no one needs lessons to eat, especially dancers . . . especially after a particularly grueling class or rehearsal! We're hungry, so we eat.

Now, moving from our hands as the primary method of eating to using a utensil such as a knife and fork is a learned behavior. Ever see a young child using a fork the first time?

Riding a bike usually takes lessons, doesn't it? Learning to drive takes lessons as well. Even those born with a good voice usually take singing lessons. We take lessons to ski, to play tennis, to bowl, to do a multitude of things, physical and otherwise. Most activities we take for granted in our adulthood were skills that required a process of learning and practice in our childhood. For sure, some activities need more lessons than others and some of us need more lessons than others to learn a given skill, but lessons nonetheless are required.

Not so simply put . . . learning anything takes someone showing us (a form of teaching), then lots of practice on our part (what good students do), then someone correcting and re-showing us (more teaching), and lots more practice on our part (more good student behavior) before it (whatever the desired learned skill is) becomes easy enough for us to do and maybe even appear "natural", as if we never needed lessons in the first place.

Oh the humanity . . .

The interesting and sometimes frustrating thing to note is that being able to execute a skill "easily" and "naturally" keeps others from ever realizing how hard you actually worked to learn that skill. Most people will never really know the amount of time you spent or the blood, sweat, and tears you've shed (especially in the area of dance or any athletic endeavor) to learn the skills you have that everyone now thinks you do so easily.

That's the dilemma we all have as skilled artists and athletes. We want everyone to believe that making those three-pointers with the basketball is an everyday natural occurrence. We want people to believe that the masterpiece they so astutely perceive we painted was something that just oozed out of us. We want the crowds screaming "Bravo, Bravo" to believe that our uncanny ability to turn, jump and move across the stage with astounding beauty is because we have been blessed by the artistic "gods". Then when they do believe we are as special as we want them to believe, we are left with mixed feelings because our years of work and dedication never really get acknowledged. Oh the humanity!

Warning! - Entering a no fun zone!

Three biggest misconceptions about dance . . .

There is a great irony in that the three primary reasons people begin dancing are also the three primary misconceptions people have about the learning to dance process. It only takes a student one or two attempts in a dance class to find out that the perceived fun they were absolutely certain they witnessed in a dance concert, music video, television special, film or stage production -- which is what attracted and enticed them to take dance classes in the first place -- seems to be missing. Where'd it go? What happened?

Over the years I have seen many young (and not so young) students become bewildered, disenchanted and completely turned off to technique classes after only a few attempts. You see, they, like most people, were under the misguided notion that taking dance classes was sure to be about the most fun activity a person could do. After all, that is how the dancers they saw on the stage or television made it look. Weren't those dancers they saw on stage turning, kicking, and jumping themselves into some sort of euphoric, ecstatic, ecstasy? Weren't those dancers in the music video having the time of their lives? Well, weren't they?

NEWSFLASH! It's the professional's job to make what they do look effortless and, yes, sometimes even fun, even when -- especially when -- it's not!
Here's the thing . . .

THiNG # 11

THE NUMBER ONE MiSCONCEPTiON ABOUT DANCE iS THAT iT'S FUN!

More precisely, that the learning process of dance is fun. Dancing can be fun at times, but, learning to dance requires an enormous commitment of time, energy and hard work to acquire the requisite skills necessary in order to actually begin dancing!

Before you get all upset at me for taking the fun out of dance, let's understand what fun is.

• • DEFiNiTiON TiME • •

Fun is a mental and physical vacation from all things stressful. It's a day without responsibility, a day without work and, most certainly, a day without anyone pushing, prodding, and critiquing you. That's certainly not what happens in a dance class, is it?

Over the years, I've had many a student come up to me after having a particularly difficult time in class to express their concerns on how I cannot possibly understand how tough it is for them to grasp what's going on because dancing comes so easily to me. As if my birth experience was one of leaping out of the womb, doing a double tour en l'air, and landing in a perfect split position right in the doctor's hand. (Don't let this get around, but I missed the doctor's hand by just this much.)

I explain to her or him that what the frustrated, even irritated, student is experiencing is common to all. It's what everyone, even the most talented, goes through.

The principle reason dancing looks like fun is because those who do it well make it look easy. After all, something that's seemingly performed so effortlessly can't be all that difficult to learn, can it? That's what many young (and not so young) students believe, and therein lies the problem. Here's the thing . . .

THiNG # 12

THE NUMBER TWO MiSCONCEPTiON ABOUT DANCE iS THAT iT'S EASY!

To be more precise, that it's easy to learn. Learning to dance requires an immense commitment, with a great amount of tenacity to keep on keeping on in order to work through the difficult times, of which there are many.

Many students are completely taken aback when they experience what is required of them their very first class. The dance exercises alone are often enough to send the first timer into a state of cataclysmic shock. You see it written all over their faces . . . why is this so difficult, and where's the blasted fun?

That brings us to the third misconception people have about dance. It's something that generally hits the new student the day after their first class and continues to hit them as long as they continue training. It's inevitable, and believe me, everyone who's ever trained to be a dancer has experienced it. Here's the thing . . .

THiNG # 13

THE NUMBER THREE MiSCONCEPTiON ABOUT DANCE iS THAT iT'S PAIN-FREE!

Dancing is one of the most intense, physically demanding endeavors a "body" could ever pursue. It takes an inordinate amount of physical, mental, and emotional effort. Not unlike most athletic ventures, what one is required to do in a dance class is beyond what any mere "mortal" could ever imagine.

So what am I saying . . . that dancing is extremely difficult, absolutely no fun, and on top of that, it hurts? The answer depends on how good you want to get and how far you want to go. For those who really wish to pursue a career in dance, or who truly desire to become accomplished, the answer is yes, pretty much, and yes. Yes, it's extremely difficult to learn; yes, though it can at times be fun, it's often a struggle; and, as I tell my students, I haven't been without some kind of pain for over 40 years!

When I see the look of agony begin to appear on the faces of my students, I try to ease their discomfort by informing them that: **"The pain you feel is your own!"** **(Dennonism #5)**

Understand now, I'm not talking about the kind of pain one has when a bone is sticking out of the skin, and there's blood squirting out all over the place. I'm talking about the everyday, natural occurrence of "pain" that accompanies any athlete who's working to develop his or her physical capabilities beyond the "norm". This kind of pain, which is really muscle fatigue, soreness, and the like, is simply a result of the great amount of stress one is required to put on one's body, i.e. muscles, tendons, ligaments, and bones, not to mention one's brain, in order to grow. This kind of pain is a not so gentle reminder that one has been working to their fullest capacity.

Dancers (athletes of all kinds) need to understand, appreciate, and yes, even embrace the "pain" their bodies are experiencing. If learning to dance were entirely fun, incredibly easy, and totally pain-free, then there'd be many more great dancers in the world. In fact, there are relatively few great dancers—many good ones, a hoard of mediocre ones, but very few that could be categorized as great.

The process of learning to dance (learning anything) is this: First comes the work, which makes possible the learning, which produces the results, which in turn excites and motivates the student to continue to work hard, if not increase it, in order to obtain more results, which again excites the student, and on and on it goes.

I know there are going to be a whole lot of people (especially other dance instructors) who will be upset with me for taking the fun out of dance. Once again, I'm not saying there is never any fun to be had in dance. What I am saying, and what I've been building up to, is that "fun" is simply the wrong word to use in conjunction with learning anything as difficult as dance. There is another word, a far better word that is infinitely more accurate.

It's really joy, not fun, you're experiencing . . .

During all the years I was performing, there were always those who commented on all the fun I must have been having. Most of the time, especially in the early days, I'd just let it slide because I didn't want to burst their delusion that dancing on stage, in films, or television must be just about the most stress-free fun a person can possibly have. The average non-dancer wants to believe that everyone who dances is always having a great time and, unlike their work, which is "real" work, the dancer's work, and even life itself is really not work at all . . . it's fun.

Dance students need to understand the truth. Hear me, I'm not talking about the 3-to-7-year olds who are taking a once-a-week class, the purpose of which is more to develop their motor and social skills than to learn to dance. I'm not even talking about older students who are taking a once or twice-a-week Hip-Hop or Jazz class in order to be with friends and feel connected to current pop culture. I'm talking about anyone who steps into a serious learning/training environment where the purpose of the class is to actually train students toward the eventual goal of becoming a professional, or at least really good!

When it comes to a show I performed in, here's what I tell my students (I don't bother with the general public because, as I said, it would burst their delusional fantasy): "Don't ask me if I had fun, ask me if I enjoyed myself." The answer is always a resounding yes. I have great joy when I'm dancing in any capacity. Whether I'm performing, rehearsing, taking class, teaching, or choreographing, I generally experience a good deal of joy. Whether I'm in a period of enormous growth, or stagnated on some plateau I can't seem to get off, there's still a sense of joy. What am I, some kind of weirdo? No weirder than anyone who's ever trained seriously at any athletic or artistic endeavor.

Understanding joy . . .

Whereas fun is fleeting, and mostly emotion-driven, joy, on the other hand, is lasting and much deeper. Joy comes from a knowing, a deep understanding of, the purpose or result of one's efforts. No matter how tough or difficult a training/work session may be, joy is what one experiences because they know that what they're doing is moving them forward, closer to their desired goal. Joy also comes from real accomplishment. It comes as a result of a job well done. There is real joy to be had from knowing that one has completed an assignment, project or chore, no matter how difficult it was even when there was no "fun" to be had during the process. Strange as it may seem, often, the greater the difficulty, the greater the joy.

Because fun is a fleeting emotion, it does little to motivate one to work hard. As a matter of fact, fun is more a result of goofing off, than it is of hard work. Joy can be had when there is no fun in sight. It's what keeps the artist (or anyone) working, continually striving to improve his or her skills, knowing it's only through their work that they'll achieve growth and/or success.

Have I still not convinced you yet that "fun" is the wrong word? Let me ask you this. Does anyone ever ask the surgeon if the 6-hour operation that he or she just performed was fun? I don't think I want the surgeon having fun while holding my brains in his or her hands! How about asking the accountant after a very long, grueling tax season how much fun they had? What about the other arts? Does anyone ask the painter if they had fun while creating their masterpiece? Maybe cutting off his ear was part of the "fun ritual" Van Gogh used while painting. How much fun do you think Michelangelo had while lying on his back, on a splintered wood scaffolding no less, for hours on end, day-after-day, for years, painting the Sistine Chapel?

The truth is, most all professionals and artists experience a great sense of joy while working at their chosen profession, but fun, I don't think so!

A hippo makes a life-changing decision . . .

The most fun I ever had was when I was just starting out and I had yet to make a real commitment. I had a blast doing concerts and musicals in high school. There was little pressure as we were all amateurs with various levels of training. I also had a tremendous amount of fun the two Christmases I worked at Disneyland. Both times, I was cast in the annual parade as part of the Fantasia unit. One year, I was a dancing hippopotamus and the next year I was a crocodile.

When doing the parade, the most fun, and scary, times were when it rained. The ground was slippery and with each step we were at risk of falling. I remember peering through my oversized hippo head to see one of my cohorts sliding down an incline, arms flailing about, and eventually falling. It became funnier because the costume was so bulky, it was impossible to get up. The very sight of a Hippo in a tutu swinging his arms and legs about trying to get up was nothing short of hysterical. I was in tears laughing. Those who fell always had to be helped back on their feet by one of the parade monitors, and even that was funny.

Now, as much fun as I had being a part of the goofy Fantasia unit, behind my smiling, even laughing hippo face, was a seriously disenchanted human. You see, what I really wanted was to be a part of the more prestigious Mary Poppins unit. Only the best dancers were cast in that unit as they got to do the famous chimney sweep dance. They were the featured dancers in the parade—they were the stars. It was during those two Christmases at Disneyland that I came to realize a very important truth. I wasn't going to be one of the featured performers as long as I was only having fun. It was time to get serious, real serious.

Seems weird to say, doesn't it? The day I made a real commitment to becoming a professional dancer was the day the fun ended . . . or at least took a back seat to my approach to training.

Backstage at Disneyland 1969
Dennon preparing for the
annual Christmas parade

It's not my intention to discourage anyone from taking dance classes, so please don't get me wrong—fun can be had, but at some point, you too will come face to face with a decision. Do I just want to continue having fun, or do I want to get good? The truth is that fun simply cannot be counted on to help sustain one's commitment to learning anything, especially something as difficult as dance. If it's fun times alone you're out for, great, have at it, but forget about becoming any good, or, as I tell my students, if it is fun you're after, then work hard anyway, because it's more fun when you're good!

Sicilian guy Steven Peck had a unique perspective concerning the work process. He used to say: **"Enjoy your struggle!" (Steven's saying #2)** Notice, he didn't say to have fun and whistle while you work—leave that to Dopey and his gang. I really like that saying because it acknowledges that there will be a struggle and, as he puts it, the struggle is yours. Own it, and then enjoy it. If you can keep a sense of joy while you're struggling, though you may experience tough times, you will not be defeated. There's always joy to be found in the work process. Hmm, sounds like a metaphor for life to me.

Back to what dance is . . .

Unlike other artists, dancers are every bit as much athletes as any athlete. No professional or aspiring professional athlete works physically harder than his or her dancer counterpart. **"Of all the arts, dance is the only one that is both art and sport!" (Dennonism #6)**

I actually believe that dancers must work even harder, because of the artistry involved. If the ball player can hit the ball it matters not what he or she looks like. For the dancer, it does. For the basketball player who can sink baskets from all over the court, it matters not how he or she does it. For the dancer who performs equally, if not more demanding skills, it does. It also matters how they emotionally express themselves as well as how they connect to the music, the other performers, and the audience.

I'm not saying that learning to dance takes more commitment or practice than any other art. What I am saying is that learning to dance requires a physicality that the other arts simply do not. The painter is pretty much quiet and still while creating his or her art. The musician practices for hours on end, sitting down. So too the writer sits for hours at a time at the computer. The singer and actor usually get to move around a bit, but that movement could hardly be considered athletic. It is the dancer, and the dancer alone, whose physical training mirrors that of any world-class athlete. Why? Because, unlike all other artists, the dancer's body is their instrument.

Another thing to note in contrasting the dancer to all other artists is that the painter/artist, musician/artist, writer/artist, and actor/artist can continue practicing their art well into their "mature" years. Sometimes their very best work is done when they've reached those golden years. Once again, the dancer's career mirrors that of the athlete. Most dancers have to stop by the time they've reached their mid-30s. Some, if they've reached a certain notoriety, can continue their career a bit further. For the sheer joy of it, one can continue dancing into their mature years, but not professionally. The dancer's instrument, like that of the athlete, simply wears out. You don't see many 40-plus-year-olds running in the Olympics. You don't see many 40-plus-year-olds playing football or baseball . . . not professionally anyway.

For the most part, dancing is a young person's game. The dancer either has to transition to becoming a choreographer or teacher (which relatively few do) or leave the arts completely and do something else. Just like most athletes, who at some point cannot compete with their younger counterparts, the dancer's career is limited by his or her physical capabilities. Unlike pro golfers, we dancers don't have a senior tour.

Low art on the totem pole . . .

Now that I've contrasted the art of dance to the other arts, I wish to express my dismay that the art (and sport) of dance is usually placed lowest on the proverbial arts totem pole. It is, by far, physically the most difficult art to achieve any high level of competency, with the shortest potential life span, and yet it gets the least respect. I've even found that other artists (I won't mention musicians, actors, singers, painters, etc. by name) often give dance little recognition for its contribution to the art world, the theater world, and humankind. It is also the least valued in the area of money. Dancers are generally paid less than others. On any given television special or awards show, there'll be a singer (sometimes only mediocre) surrounded by professional dancers whose job it is to make the singer (who doesn't move nearly as well) look good. The singer makes millions and the dancers get athlete's feet.

So why does anybody dance? As I said, it's a calling. In the celebrated film, *The Red Shoes*, ballerina Moira Shearer was asked that very question. Her answer was simple, direct, and spoken like any true artist. Her response was, "Why do you live?"

You see, dancers -- real dancers -- simply have to express the talents they've been gifted with, or they're not fully experiencing life. For the artist, exercising or expressing one's gift serves to nourish the soul. For Sayhber and me, it's how we worship God. Every port de bras we do, and every dance step we take, is an act of praise and giving thanks. For us, it's like breath, and life, and an elaborate, all-you-can-eat barbecue feast all in one. Go figure.

Jazz Dancers, Inc. 1982 - Performance Photo: Judy Francesconi
Sayhber Rawles

CHAPTER FOUR
STYLE VERSUS TECHNIQUE
WHAT'S THE "DIFF" AND WHO CARES?

"It's been scientifically proven that those who breathe live twice as long as those who don't!" I was hired once again by the great choreographer/director Michael Kidd to assist him on a Janet Jackson music video, entitled *Alright With Me.* This was back in 1990. He had been asked by Janet to conceptualize the story that would be used to create the mini-film. We were once again on the back lot of Universal Studios (the first time was for the *Baryshnikov In Hollywood* Television Special) pulling a couple of all-nighters. In addition to the talented Ms. Jackson, there were to be cameo performances by three of musical theater's iconic stars, including Cyd Charisse, who I spoke about in the previous chapter, the great bandleader/scat singer from the 1930s and 40s, Cab Calloway, and the spectacular dance team, the Nicholas Brothers.

At one point, while waiting their turn to be filmed, I was to help the Nicholas Brothers rehearse their section. If you don't know, you should, the Nicholas Brothers were two of the most astounding dancers and performers the world has ever seen. Their athleticism, artistry, and innovation made them much more than just brilliant hoofers. Check out any one of their films and you'll be totally amazed.

While we were talking, Fayard, the older of the two, took such pride in revealing to me that he and younger brother Harold had worked very hard on interjecting artistry in their dancing. As only the Nicholas Brothers could do, he stretched out his arms and hands in the most beautiful and elegant manner demonstrating the style and grace they were very well known for. Wow . . . that was it—what he did right there was the famous smooth, trademarked arm gesture you see in all their films. It was so very clear that they had worked hard to become more than just technically proficient at what they did . . . they had real style!

Distinguishing Technique From Style . . .

I've heard many, over the years, use the terms "Ballet" and "Technique" interchangeably as if there were no distinction to be made. "Your technique is quite good"; and, "She has a very clean technique", are examples. These are all fine observations, except every time the person used the word technique, what they were thinking was Ballet technique.

In this chapter, I'm setting out to clarify the meaning of the word technique, as well as the word style, and explore how they interrelate. They are two distinct words with two distinct meanings that, on occasion, share a foothold (pun intended) on a given dance discipline.

Periodically we'll ask our students what the two words in question mean, and how exactly do they pertain to dance. Most everyone has a pretty good idea of what "style" is, but the word "technique", that's a different story. The response is pretty much that technique generally refers to things they've learned in the Ballet class like plies, tendues, pirouettes, and/or the principles of placement and alignment. Then I ask, what about what you're learning in Modern class—don't you learn any of those things there? That causes them to think. Then I ask, what about what you're learning in your Jazz class? Their response is something like: "Since Jazz is so movement oriented, and every teacher is so different, it can only be thought of as a style." So I ask, what about your Ballroom class or Tap class? Then I get a response like: "Well, you don't really learn about placement in those classes, or do pirouettes, or have to balance endlessly on one leg, so they can't really be considered technique classes." How about Hip-Hop, I ask? That one really does it. Their expression says it all: "What . . . technique in Hip-Hop class?"

It has become clear to me that because so many dancers believe the word technique is directly related first to the discipline of Ballet and then to the discipline of Modern it's hard for them to believe that Jazz dance, or any of the other dance forms, can be considered any kind of real "technique". The key word here is "can". I'll explain as we go along. Keep reading.

• • DEFiNiTiON TiME • •

Technique: A scientific, systematic method or procedure in learning or doing anything.

Style: Personal characteristics or traits interjected into something one does.

You'll notice the definition of the word "technique" does not reference Ballet at all. It actually doesn't refer to any specific activity—artistic, athletic, or otherwise. You'll also notice that the word "style" has no method or process connected to it. Style is a personal thing that is unique to each individual. Each are completely different words that, in the world of dance, continuously interrelate, sometimes to the point of confusion.

First let me break down the differences in what I call the big "T" (proper noun) Techniques and the small "t" techniques. Then I'll get into how these came about. Both words are nouns, but one is ever so "proper". As I see it, there are four possible ways to use and understand the word technique as it pertains to dance. Hang on, this explanation is going to get a bit bumpy.

The first designation refers to a main category or discipline, i.e., Ballet, Modern, Jazz, Tap, Ballroom, Latin, Hip-Hop, etc. The second way to use the word would be to distinguish one particular discipline from another within the main category. For instance, the English Royal Academy of Dancing (RAD) method is a sub-category of the main category Ballet. Capiche? The third way would be to describe the various exercises one uses to teach and train students in order to learn a particular sub-category designation. The fourth way to use the word would be to describe a teacher's method of conducting class, as well as the teacher's approach to giving and explaining exercises.

Isn't that fourth way of describing technique just the teacher's style? Sometimes. But for some teachers, their procedures and methods actually become a structured system (that's what makes it a technique) -- an effective formula, if you will -- that a teacher has developed over time (usually a long time), which proves itself to work effectively and efficiently in communicating, teaching, and training students.

Maybe I can better demonstrate the four technique categories like this:

Ballet

1. Big "T"   Main Category: Ballet Dance
2. Big "T"   Subcategory Designation: RAD Method; Cecchetti Method; Russian Method, etc.
3. Little "t" Learning techniques: Placement; Port de bras; Barre Work; Center Work; Turns, etc.
4. Little "t" Instructional techniques: Developed method or system (formula) of instructing/training

Modern

1. Big "T"   Main Category: Modern Dance
2. Big "T"   Subcategory Designation: Graham Method; Limon Method; Humphrey Method, etc.
3. Little "t" Learning techniques: Placement; Port de bras; Floor Work; Contractions; Falls, etc.
4. Little "t" Instructional techniques: Developed method or system (formula) of instruction/training

Jazz

1. Big "T" Main Category: Jazz Dance
2. Big "T" Subcategory Designation: Cole Method; Luigi Method; Rawles Method, etc.
3. Little "t" Learning Techniques: Placement; Port de bras; Isolations; Standing and Floor Work, etc.
4. Little "t" Instructional techniques: Developed method or system (formula) of instructing/training

The same breakdown can be made in other, non-dance disciplines such as:

Martial Arts

1. Big "T" Main Category: Martial Arts
2. Big "T" Subcategory Designation: Tae Kwon Do; Karate; Kung Fu, etc.
3. Little "t" Learning Techniques: Forms/Routines/Katas; Fighting techniques, etc.
4. Little "t" Instructional techniques: Developed method or system (formula) of instructing/training

To understand how these different uses of the word "technique" came about we must now slide on over to "style". The word itself is much easier for everyone to comprehend. It's a word we hear everyday as it permeates popular culture. Everyone is looking to have style, or create his or her own personal style. At least that's what most people think, they think they want. What actually happens, what usually happens, since most people want to "belong", is they copy, imitate, and embrace someone else's style, regardless of how it makes them look (but I digress).

Simply explained, style is one's individual personality that is interjected, and subsequently revealed, in his or her dancing or teaching or choreography or, actually, anything one does or says. Your style, my style, everyone's style is revealed in the way we dress, the way we walk, and even in the way we talk, and most certainly in the way we dance. Okay, that's style, but how does that interrelate to technique? Good question.

Personal style necessitates the development of techniques . . .

The ultimate goal of the originator of a new style is to have others understand and completely digest the meanings behind any and all movements the creator "invents", so the creator has dancers who are able to bring to life his or her vision the way he or she envisions it. The most efficient way to do this is to create methods, i.e. techniques, which convey the style.

Here's the thing . . .

THiNG # 14

IT TAKES "TECHNiQUES" TO TEACH A "STYLE"!

When a creative artist develops a personal style, or new "language", and doesn't want to be the only one who can do it, it becomes necessary to develop techniques in order to teach others not only the external movements but also the reasons and meanings behind the movements.

These codified exercises form the basis of one's teaching techniques that can lead to the formation of a bona fide big "T" Technique.

Example One: Ballet - Its aristocratic beginnings . . .

As I briefly explained in the previous chapter, Ballet grew out of a social/court dance that was performed for and with royalty in France in the sixteenth and seventeenth centuries. The word ballet is a French word taken from the Italian balletto, which is from the Latin ballare, which means "to dance". At its core, the word ballet simply means to dance. One must understand that court dances were not the dances of the masses or the peasants. Rather, they were the dances of the elites. Those that were allowed into the "courts" of royalty thought themselves to be super-important, highly sophisticated, and, très élégant.

The dances these elites participated in were made up of linear movements that traveled side to side as well as forward and back. To accentuate the sophistication of the dance the erudite participants would stiffen their backs and hold their heads (and noses) up high in a rather "snooty" fashion. This became the "style" of the dance. It soon became evident it was much easier to accomplish the lateral gliding and sliding of one's feet along the floor with a "turned out" leg and foot position. Those that didn't, might find themselves tripping over themselves, falling head over heels, landing at the feet of the highly bemused King.

In order to facilitate the learning of the preferred way or "style" of the dance, it became practical to develop certain methods (little "t" techniques I call them). The turned out feet and legs, along with gracefully executed arm movements, all topped off with an extremely lifted, turned up nose became the first little "t" techniques that were taught to anyone wanting to avoid the potential wrath of the King.

Exercises were developed in order to teach the prospective participant the accepted, "proper" way to execute a given movement or step. Basically what happened was, over time, there developed a method to the madness. A codified naming and numbering system for every conceivable position developed, which became the standardized techniques used in every Ballet class the world over. It took a while, but over the course of hundreds of years, we went from a highly stylized, social/court dance to a very formalized dance art/technique form called Ballet.

George Balanchine, credited by many as the "father" of American Ballet, is a perfect example of someone whose individual style evolved to become what is known the world aver as the Balanchine Technique. An immigrant from Russia, he set out to create a school in America where he could train strong dancers to dance his particular way, i.e. *style*.

In 1934, he opened the School of American Ballet in New York City. He eventually formed the Ballet Society dance company, which eventually became the highly accalimed New York City Ballet. He was noted for having reworked basic ballet movements, such as port de bras and arabesques, in such a way so to satisfy his vision of how they should be presented. His super-quick jumps often didn't allow for landing with one's heels fully touching the floor. Over time his techniques became codified to such a degree that others (mostly those trained by him) could also teach his techniques using his methods.

For 35 years, George Balanchine was synonymous with New York City Ballet. The Balanchine Technique is so recognizable the world over, it's impossible for a City Ballet dancer to go unrecognized.

Example Two: Modern - Its rebellious beginnings . . .

Simply put, Modern Dance was born out of a desire to not be Ballet. In the early part of the 20th century, Isadora Duncan was known as a "free form" dancer. "Free form", as in no forced upon, pre-determined rules or "techniques" to adhere to. To her, ballet was unnatural and therefore, even ugly. Imagine that—thinking Ballet was ugly? Her dancing was to be free of all artificial, unnatural constructs. She abandoned the tutus, threw away the pointe shoes, and embraced her "natural", sometimes naked (that's literal as well as metaphorical) self.

This is the woman who many call the "mother" of modern dance. She led a rather unconventional life, especially for that time. As it does for everyone, her approach to life informed her approach to dancing. Though she relished in her free-form approach to life and dancing, she too found it necessary to develop actual methods or procedures (some would call them techniques) in order to teach her students how to be free. Ironic isn't it? She needed to develop small "t" techniques in order to get across to her students the "way" she wanted them to dance. Small "t" techniques aside, what Isadora Duncan really developed was more of a dance "philosophy". She wanted to share her ideas on how to emotionally express oneself in the arena of physical movement, but did not want to bog anyone down with too many rules to follow.

Though Duncan's "philosophy" never quite developed into a big "T" "Technique", her ideas of a freer form of dance did endure. Around the same time, Ruth St. Denis along with her husband Ted Shawn developed the world-renowned dance company, Denishawn. It wasn't to be old-fashioned classical Ballet; it was a new, modern way of dancing, hence the term Modern. It became for them, as it does for everyone, necessary to develop methods -- meaning "techniques" -- in order to teach their dancers their particular way of dancing.

St. Denis had a real affinity for certain ethnic dances such as those categorized as "East Indian". Her techniques reflected that. The Denishawn dancers led the way for many of the big names in Modern Dance that followed—Graham, Humphrey, Weidman, and Limon to name a few. Each of these pioneers of Modern developed their own, highly structured methods and procedures -- yes, that means "techniques" -- to teach the next generation of dancers exactly what they wanted from them.

Martha Graham, probably the most famous of early Modern Dance pioneers, is a prime example of how someone's individual "style" begat techniques that eventually become known as a big "T" Technique. Graham didn't just want to make up dances. What she endeavored to do was develop her own, new "language" of movement. Her personal "style" necessitated developing techniques. These took on the form of a uniquely developed set of exercises that she put together in a routine that her dancers would work over and over again all for the sole purpose of training them to stand, move, port de bras, stretch, contract, isolate, lift, extend, fall, etc., exactly as she wished them to do. Her routine of exercises, i.e. techniques, became the "vocabulary" of movement from which she would draw upon to choreograph. To this day the Graham Technique is easily recognizable as well as highly regarded among dance aficionados.

Example Three: Jazz - Its evolutionary beginnings . . .

The Jazz class structure evolved into what we know today because of early dance pioneers. Most notably, a man named Jack Cole who is often credited as being the "father" of Jazz dance. In the late 1920s, Cole began training and performing with Modern Dance pioneers Ruth St. Denis and Ted Shawn in the highly acclaimed Denishawn Company. He later went on to work with Shawn in his equally successful all-male dance group. After being let go for being habitually late and disrespectful to Shawn, Cole went to work with two other former Denishawn defectors, Doris Humphrey and Charles Weidman.

The Humphrey-Weidman Company performed in concert venues as well as in nightclubs. Cole was considered a very good dancer but, due to reasons one can only speculate, his tardiness and lack of respect for the directors once again caused him to be dismissed. It was at this point he decided to go out on his own and go "commercial" so he could not only fulfill his artistic needs, but also make enough money to support himself and his dancers.

There is a bit of irony, as he, a man known for being late all the time, became quite the taskmaster, never tolerating any behavior like he had been known for. He took the training he received, which included certain ethnic dances like Middle Eastern, and explored his own way of movement and expression to the contemporary music of his day, which was called Jazz. His unique blending of techniques and rhythms went over well in the various nightclubs they performed in. Always wishing to expand his knowledge and be current with the times, he sought out and studied what was going on in the African-American communities, which ultimately made its way into his work.

Though people refer to Cole's work as Jazz, he actually preferred the term "Theater Dance" to describe what he was doing. It was dance designed for theater, or theatrical presentation. He developed a uniquely personal method of marrying movement with the music of the day, and presented it in a "commercial" venue to a larger audience than he would have in a concert setting. It was someone else who coined the term "Jazz Dance" for the simple reason the music he used fell into the Jazz category.

This is why Jazz dance's closest relative is Modern. The disciplines share a common heritage. Jazz and Modern use the same positions, movements, off-balance falls, and floor work. Where they part company is in the connection they make to the music.

After gaining notoriety for his work in nightclubs, Broadway, and film, he earned enough clout to get Harry Cohn, the head of Columbia Pictures, to allow him to have the first and, subsequently, the only company of contract dancers at a major Hollywood Studio. While there, he continued to define and refine his "way" by developing specific technique exercises his dancers would have to work over and over again. These dancers would eventually become the standard bearers for which all other dancers who worked for him had to measure up. Among them were such notables as Carol Haney (who would later assist Bob Fosse), Matt Mattox, and Gwen Verdon (who later married Fosse and also helped him develop his own style).

Utilizing his own personal approach (small "t" technique), Cole was able to train his dancers in his Method (big "T" Technique), utilizing the exercises (small "t" techniques) he developed, so they'd be ready for any film that he might be assigned to do. Because of the development of Cole (big "T") Technique, unlike other Hollywood choreographers, he had a nucleus of well-trained dancers, at the ready, that were capable of doing what he wanted, exactly in the style he wanted.

The training methods, i.e. techniques, he developed in order to teach his particular style led the way for many others. Classes in the newly established Jazz dance idiom sprang up all over the place. His exciting, dynamic work couldn't help but influence other theater dance icons, such as Bob Fosse and Gene Kelly. Unfortunately, he's a man most dancers today have never heard of, but he's worth investigating further on your own to better understand the rich history of Jazz/Theater dance and it's connection to Modern and certain ethnic/folk dances. Look for a biography of Cole, entitled, *Unsung Genius*, by Glen Loney.

Tracking the technique/style confusion . . .

Jack Cole aside, to most people's way of thinking, Jazz dance can never really be a genuine Technique, for it relies so heavily on an individual's personality and/or personal approach, or "feel", to express it. Therefore, it can only be thought of as a "style". That's partially true because, unlike Ballet, or even certain forms of Modern, there's nothing universal about it.

The truth is, wherever you go in the world, when you take a Jazz class you're going to get something different. Forget the world, Jazz classes within the same studio often have little in common. There seems to be no two Jazz teachers that teach the same techniques the same way. For the student it can be a little unsettling to realize that what you learned in one Jazz class may not be of help to you in another. To the extent one does find anything similar, it would be in the use of certain dance terminology.

All dance disciplines borrow heavily from the Ballet world to describe its positions and movements. Both the Modern and Jazz dancer will use terms like plié, tendue, attitude and arabesque. There will be differences in their approach to doing these positions or movements, but the terminology is the same.

I believe this is a major source of the confusion in the thinking that Ballet is the only real big "T" Technique and all others are not. Let me clear that thinking up. Just because all forms of dance use Ballet terminology to describe their positions or movements, does not mean that there are no clear-cut differences.

Unlike Ballet, there has never been nor is there likely ever to be, a universally codified accepted set of rules, standards and terminology that govern Jazz dance. Though Jazz dance is embraced the world over, its allure seems to be that individuals are allowed to originate movements and connect those movements to a particular piece of music in a highly personal way.

It's the same for Jazz musicians and how they use their instruments to make music in a highly personal way. That's not to say there is no structure or form to it. Musicians could never play together if everyone ignored everyone else. Musicians must develop their skills to such a high degree that they are able to play with a sense of emotional freedom, all the while staying in sync with the other musicians in the group.

Here's the thing . . .

THiNG # 15

JAZZ DANCE, LiKE JAZZ MUSiC, BEGS FOR PERSONAL iNTERPRETATiON!

More so than Ballet and Modern, Jazz dance relies heavily on one's own personal interpretation and connection to the music. That's style! That's the beauty of Jazz dance. It begs for one to soulfully connect the movement to the music.

As I tell my students: **"It's been scientifically proven that those who breathe live twice as long as those who don't!" (Dennonism #7)** It's that breathing life into a dance that keeps one from merely being a robot. In other words, from being strictly a technician practitioner. Breathing life into something, be it music, dance, a song, a play, or whatever, means digging deep into one's soul and allowing it to be revealed. That's real style. A performer's job is first to find, and then to release that which makes him or her unique.

That's exactly why every Jazz teacher/choreographer is different from another. Those differences are directly related to the differences all individuals have with one another. Everyone is shaped by their training and experience as well as one's basic personality, which is influenced to a greater or lesser degree by genetics, family, relationships, geography, shoe size and inseam. Inseam? Yes, taller people with longer legs tend to dance bigger and a tad slower than those who are on the shorter side, who tend to dance sharper and quicker. Those with exceptionally big feet, trip a lot, so they incorporate a lot of floor work in their choreography.

Osmosis over technique . . .

Not everyone who teaches develops techniques to teach their style. It is my experience that most dance teachers do not "teach" their style. A lot of teachers (especially, but not limited to, Jazz and Modern) don't really understand their own way of doing things. What? Yes, they're more akin to the artists I talked about in Chapter One who work more intuitively than analytically. They dance the way they dance and know not why.

I've personally seen many a teacher whose skills in the area of actual instruction are quite limited. They show what they want and mumble some pretty incoherent things and then, to top it off, get upset when the student doesn't understand. These kinds of "teachers" may themselves be talented dancers, or even skilled choreographers, but they're certainly not very good teachers.

To the extent that anyone does pick up this teacher's style, it is only through a kind of osmosis, which is to say, a slow, gradual process of unconscious assimilation. The truth is if you're around somebody long enough, you'll begin to take on his or her characteristics. A student who spends years with a teacher will eventually begin to dance like that teacher. Their dance "styles" will be similar, but the student -- not being the originator of the style -- doesn't really understand what he or she is doing, or why.

Conclusion . . .

So, when does a style become a technique? When the originator develops and codifies specific exercises that effectively teach that style which would include understanding the originator's intent. When does a teacher's methods of instructing become a technique? When that teacher develops tried-and-true methods that prove, over time, to be understandable, reliable and, most importantly, effective.

No doubt many will quibble with me on the use of the word Technique and would prefer the word "Method". Whether you want to call it the Balanchine Method or Technique, or the Graham Method or Technique, or the Cole Method or Technique, doesn't really matter to me. Either way -- Method or Technique -- it still encompasses a clearly defined, structured set of exercises that leads one to a clearly defined end/purpose— that is to dance a certain, specific way.

On a personal note . . .

Sayhber and I have often been asked what particular "Style" or "Technique" of Jazz we teach. They're usually wondering if we teach a Modern-based Jazz, or Commercial (a term which is pretty meaningless), or if we teach "Fosse", or maybe we like to teach whatever the current fad that happens to be popular at that moment. Our Technique is Classical in nature in that it draws on the "Fathers" of Jazz/Musical Theater: Jack Cole, Bob Fosse, Jerome Robbins, Luigi, as well as our mentor, Steven Peck. Add to the mix our own life experiences (point of view), and you've got us!

We had our own company in the L.A. area for 13 years. It was called Jazz Dancers, Inc., or JDI for short. It was during those years that we were able to explore our own creativity. Like anyone setting out to "find themselves", we borrowed from others, reworking exercises and techniques, developed our own exercises and techniques, and explored our own creativity as we created numerous original "Jazz Works".

Over the course of those 13 years, we developed and established our own distinct methods, i.e. techniques, of teaching and choreographing. The techniques we developed have proven themselves time and again, year after year, to be efficient ways to convey the proper execution, as we see it, of the Classical Jazz positions, arms, isolations, progressions, movement patterns, transition steps, floor work, turns and jumps. The techniques also facilitate one's understanding of a given position, or a step's origin and meaning, in order to help one grasp the intent and "feel" (as we deem it) that belongs to the step or movement. In short, we teach the Rawles, Big "T" Technique.

We're not trendy, to state the obvious. Fashions and trends are always changing. What's "hip" today is totally passé tomorrow. Classical Jazz, like Classical Ballet, is forever. Just as Classical Ballet is foundational to all Contemporary Ballet, so is Classical Jazz the basis of all other, trendier styles of Jazz. We've been teaching for a lot of years now, and have seen many trends along with many teachers come and go. Amazingly we're still at it. One thing for sure, as long as we teach a Classically-based Jazz big "T" Technique we'll never go out of "style".

Jazz Dancers, Inc. mid-1980s - Performance Photo: Unknown
Dennon Rawles

ACT TWO

It's Your Mess!
- So Clean It Up -

On the set of *Staying Alive* 1982 – Photos: Nell Alano
Top Photo: Sylvester Stallone and Dennon discussing the next shot
Bottom Photo: Dennon, Stallone, and John Travolta between takes

CHAPTER FIVE
FOUR FACTORS THAT DETERMINE SUCCESS
THE ENEMY OF GROWTH IS COMFORT!

"If it doesn't hurt, how do you know you're here?" In 1983, we were fortunate enough to have been selected to choreograph the sequel to the mega hit film,
Saturday Night Fever. Our film, *Staying Alive*, was to move John Travolta's character,
Tony, from the discothèque to the Broadway stage. It was an amazing experience to
have been chosen from all the prospective choreographers across the country to create
the dances for a major motion picture, especially one starring John Travolta and directed
by Sylvester Stallone.

I won't get into the problem we had in choreographing the big finale dance to
one song, only to have the song changed in post-production without our knowing, hence
making the choreography seem to not make sense as it didn't quite fit the music. I also
won't get into the problem of having choreographed dance sequences that would have
worked better filmed from one angle only to have it filmed from another. Whoops! Too
late—I got into it. Problems aside, working with John proved to be an important step in
our career and, to put it simply, John was and is a sweetheart of a guy.

To prepare for the film, Stallone put John on a training regimen that would have
challenged the strongest athlete. He had a professional trainer for his cardio and weight
training, which he did daily, and was placed on a special diet. He also had a private dance
instructor working with him for a couple of months prior to our coming on board. His
schedule was demanding and grueling, to say the least. As I said, we were hired to choreograph the dances and help John transition from being the great Disco dancer everybody saw in the first film to becoming a believable Broadway dancer.

I don't think he'll mind me revealing the fact that most days he was in some
kind of pain—often a lot of pain. I'm sure, at times, he thought twice or even thrice on
whether it was worth it. He, like all seriously training athletes, needed some encouragement, check that . . . lots of encouragement. That's only natural, but ultimately he understood that what went into obtaining the results he so "ached" to achieve was a determined, resolute commitment that superseded any and all physical, mental and emotional
pain. He harnessed his passion, surrounded himself with the best instructors/trainers he
could find, and set out to become . . . Tony Manero, redux.

Achieving greatness hurts! . . .
When I began this project, this book (thesis really), I contemplated using a
different title. It's another saying I use a lot: **"If it doesn't hurt, how do you know
you're here?" (Dennonism #8)** I say it all the time to my students, usually right when
they are in the middle of a particularly difficult exercise. I know the old adage "no pain,
no gain" has gone out of fashion in recent years. The problem comes down to the meaning of the word "pain". Let's face it, the word has a definite negative connotation.

Most world-class dancers, skaters, gymnasts, and athletes of all kinds understand from their own training regimens that how good they get is determined by several
factors, the most important of which is the quantity and quality of the work they put in.

Something to ponder:: **"How much effort does it take to become the world's
worst dancer?" (Dennonism #9)** The question is not meant to be profound, but it does
get at the heart of what it takes to achieve greatness. The answer of course is none,
nil, nada, zero, and a whole lot of other words that mean the same thing. It takes no
effort to be bad at anything. We all start off that way, which is to say, we all start off
knowing little or nothing about a particular subject we may want to learn.

In this chapter, I want to discuss the four factors I believe to be the ultimate determinant of one's success . . . in anything.

There are those who will argue for a fifth element, called "luck". To the degree that sometimes there are intervening events that occur, that we have little or nothing to do with, which influence an outcome of a particular endeavor we're involved in, that's true. Those unexpected influences, i.e. good or back luck, are things I prefer to call "happenstance", meaning they are just things or events that happen. They don't necessarily happen to any person, they just happen and it affects a person. Sometimes those unexpected events are things we inadvertently had something to do with—meaning we did something or said something, or didn't do something or say something that, at least in part, led to the eventual "happenstance" happening. Sometimes we have absolutely nothing to do with an event happening, even though it directly affects us. If it affects us in a positive way, we call it "good luck" and if it affects us in negative way, we call it "bad luck".

I don't really like the word "luck", because it's too often used to explain either why someone did achieve or win, or it's used to explain away someone's lack of achievement or failure to win. Either way, it's just a way of avoiding responsibility.

Leaving "luck" aside, it's important to have a good, mindful understanding of the four factors that I believe to be the actual determinant of one's success. One of them we have absolutely nothing to do with. The other three we do. They are:

1. **TALENT** – Gifts from God.
2. **PASSION/DESIRE** – The fire that fuels the desire.
3. **EXCELLENT INSTRUCTION** - An absolute must.
4. **WORK ETHIC** – It's all up to you, baby!

Factor # 1: TALENT

NEWSFLASH! **Talent is something you are born with!** It is that natural ability, capacity, skill, or artistry that one has, from birth, that cannot be explained. It's a God-given gift that none of us can take any credit (or blame) for.

Every person has certain talents or "gifts" in some or several areas. When we recognize an extraordinarily high degree of talent in children, we call them prodigies. For most people, though, one's talents may not be as readily apparent. It's only through a process of search and exploration that one discovers one's talents.

First and foremost a person's talents are found in what comes relatively easy to him or her. That comes under the heading of aptitude. Basically, it's what one is pretty good at without too much effort. For some, it may be the area of mathematics or science. For others, it could be the arena of languages and linguistics. It could be athletics and, for some others, it may be found in the crazy world of the arts.

Secondly, one's talents are found in what interests or captivates a person. It's what seems to lure one's attention away from all other things. That's why our young people need to be exposed to lots of different activities as they grow up. It's only through experiencing a variety of academic, athletic, and artistic endeavors that a person can discover what really grabs them.

My epiphany came to me when I was twelve. I was an average kid with no sense of direction or ambition. By the suggestion of my older brother to my mother, I was enrolled in a ballroom dance class. The studio was Call's Fine Arts Center in Long Beach, CA. Its major claim to fame was having produced Bobby Burgess and Barbara Boylan, the popular dance team who became featured performers on the Lawrence Welk Show. Burgess was also one of the original Mouseketeers.

I had no idea what I was getting into, but was open to the idea and soon became captivated by the experience. After a short time, I discovered I had a certain natural feel for it. I was able to pick up the steps pretty easily and, because of the positive recognition I received from my teachers and fellow classmates (especially the girls), I was encouraged to keep at it. I soon became pre-occupied with the very thought of dancing and couldn't wait to get back to class. The whole idea of dancing attracted me like nothing I had ever encountered. I was hooked and I have my big brother Dave to thank for it.

Now back to talent. It's important to understand that as essential as talent is -- and it is -- talent alone will not take you to your destination. It's simply not enough. One of my very favorite quotes is from our 30th president, Calvin Coolidge. He said, "Nothing in the world can take the place of persistence. Talent will not; nothing is more common than unsuccessful men with talent. Genius will not; unrewarded genius is almost a proverb. Education will not; the world is full of educated derelicts. Persistence and determination alone are the omnipotent. The slogan, Press On!, has solved and always will solve the problems of the human race."

Here's the thing . . .

THiNG # 16

TALENT IS ONLY THE STARTING POINT!

Talent is not the "be all", "end all" determinant of one's success. It's only the point from which we begin the process of becoming or learning whatever we wish to become or learn. Whether it be artistic, athletic, or academic, talent alone will not get you there.

There are highly talented people (in all fields) who are lazy. Lazy? Yes, because of their high, sometimes extraordinarily high, level of talent these people need only to rely on their natural abilities -- abilities that require no concerted effort -- to accomplish most tasks required of them. Their reliance on their "natural" abilities can, over time, lead to a diminished sense of urgency or ambition which can lead to laziness.

The highly talented are not alone in this regard. The minimally talented can be just as, if not more, lazy. As a matter of fact, it could be argued that the minimally talented need to work harder than their highly talented counterparts just to get to the place where the highly talented begin. No matter the level of one's talent(s), it is for certain that most people never fully develop or completely realize their gifts. Why? That very question brings us to the next three factors—the ones you do have control over.

Factor # 2: PASSION/DESIRE

Passion is a reflection of a burning desire that emanates from deep within a person. That burning desire manifests itself in an unstoppable determination to pursue something. I have known dancers who I believe to have lesser "natural talent" than others, who ultimately go further along the "success road continuum" because of their passion. I believe it to be true for all other endeavors as well. Passion can and should manifest itself into a motivating force that propels a person to continue on, no matter how difficult or frustrating it gets.

Let's say theoretically that someone has 100% potential ability in a given area and uses only half of it, and another person has 75% potential ability in the same area and uses all or most of it. Who's going to be the better dancer, or doctor, or lawyer, or etc., etc. etc.? I've seen some who are blessed with the "perfect" dance body and have a good sense of rhythm, and yet because of a limited passion, their progress slows, if not stops, well short of their potential. Rather than respecting their talents to the point of fully developing them, they rely on their "natural" ability to impress others and even get them work.

Basically, they're unresponsive to the needs of their own talents. Talent has needs? Yes, talent needs to be cultivated and worked in order to develop, grow, and thrive. I believe when someone neglects their God-given gifts, they're showing a certain amount of disrespect—both to God, the giver, and to their specific talent, the gift. That disrespect generally manifests itself in laziness.

I like what the great comedian/actor Red Skelton once said in an interview concerning his great comic ability. He referred to his talent of being funny as God's gift to him, and his making others laugh was his gift back to God. He discovered and appreciated his gift, and understood it was up to him to work it, develop it, and then share it.

The person who neglects his or her talents is not only being lazy, he or she is obliterating what could have been! Good old King Solomon, considered by many to be the wisest man who ever lived, put it this way: "He who is slothful in his work is a brother to him that is a great destroyer." Proverbs 18:9 NKJ.

Whatever the level of one's talents, it is one's passion that is the greater determinate of one's achievement. It's simple—passion trumps talent!

Factor # 3: EXCELLENT INSTRUCTION

It is absolutely crucial to the success of any student, in any subject, to have really excellent instruction by really excellent teachers who not only teach, but also motivate and inspire, as well as push, prod and probe when necessary. Later on in Act Three, we examine the qualities that make for an excellent "educator". Right now, I just want to make the point that the quality of instruction one receives has a direct correlation to the progress one makes.

No matter how naturally "gifted" a person is and how much passion and desire they may have, without someone to teach and train as well as motivate and inspire him or her, those "gifts" will likely never be fully developed.

This is where anyone just starting out faces a dilemma. Finding a good teacher when you yourself hardly know anything about the subject you want to learn can be difficult. The unfortunate truth is, with poor teaching, a student could end up worse off than if he or she never began formally studying in the first place. I come across students all the time whose poor training have actually set them back. It's as if they began at the starting line and ran backwards for fifty yards greatly increasing the distance between them and the finish line. It's not their fault, mind you. They didn't know the teacher or school they studied with for so many years would actually harm them.

So how can one tell if a school or instructor is good? Never fear, when you get into Act Three, you'll learn what to look for when determining if a school is right for you.

It's sad, but I end up with many students in my classes who are poorly trained by previous teachers who are well intentioned, I'm sure, but whose own talents and training have rendered them ill-equipped. I'm not just meaning the physical side of things, either. It's not just the lack of understanding of a dancer's placement and the technically correct execution of a given step I'm referring to. I'm talking about a real ignorance of the importance of understanding their responsibility in the teaching/learning equation. That brings us to the forth, final and, without a doubt, most important factor.

Factor # 4: WORK ETHIC

Now we're getting to where the dancer gets *on the floor*—that is to say where a person's passion manifests itself into a purposeful, determined series of actions directed toward obtaining a desired goal. I don't exactly know why or how, but for quite some time, maybe a generation or two, we as a society have been lax in our teaching the meaning of, the value of, and the absolute necessity of having what I call a "strong, personal proactive work ethic" to our youths.

The world's most prolific inventor Thomas Edison once said, "Genius is one percent inspiration and ninety-nine percent perspiration". He also said, "Opportunity is missed by most people because it is dressed in overalls and looks like work".

These days, many young ones (and not so young ones) show themselves to have greatly underdeveloped work habits. They do not know what it means to work hard or, more importantly, why they should work hard. Some of this has to do with the thinking that learning should always be fun, and you know what I think about fun.

If one is always looking for the "fun" in any given learning situation, they'll never be a high achiever. No matter how much fun something like dance or sports or anything may seem on the surface, at some point there'll come the realization that, in order to progress at it, the level and intensity of the work has to increase. Hear that? The work level has to increase! In case you don't already know this . . . the more work, the less fun.

Developing an excellent work ethic has little to do with "fun" and everything to do with the understanding that no matter how much talent one has or how wonderful the instruction is, if a student doesn't put in the necessary work, it'll all be for naught. You may even think you have a passion for something, but if you don't understand that the purpose of that passion is to motivate you to put in the work that's required, then you don't really have passion at all—you only thought you did.

What you probably have is a nominal-to-moderate interest that does little to move you past the "play at it" stage. That's okay if "playing at it" is all you want to do. Just know that playing at something will not result in great achievement.

Great achievement comes from great work. The motivation to begin and then continue that great work effort, especially during the tough times (which there always are), comes from real passion. That "real" passion is the "fire that fuels the desire" that burns deep within a person's soul, which drives one to continue to work harder than they themselves ever imagined.

Understand that nobody starts out with strong work habits. It's just not natural to the human condition. It's something that's purposely acquired over time . . . much time. It has to be learned and then continually "worked" or exercised in order to develop into a personal characteristic or trait that will serve a person in all their learning endeavors.

Parents and teachers have failed (my opinion) to get through to their students the importance of developing a "strong, personal proactive work ethic". Once again, I'll be speaking directly to instructors (and bosses and parents) about this in Act Three. It's ultimately up to each individual to work extremely hard in order to override their own natural apathetic tendencies, in order to win the battle against their own laziness. Yes, it takes hard work to become a hard worker!

Beyond the comfort zone . . .

Everybody has a certain comfort zone from which they do not like to stray. That comfort zone is a self-imposed stress ceiling or wall we all place on or around ourselves. There seems to be a certain level of stress or discomfort we'll allow ourselves to enter when learning something, but at some point we put on the brakes and decide it's just too difficult to go any further.

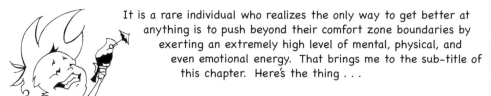

It is a rare individual who realizes the only way to get better at anything is to push beyond their comfort zone boundaries by exerting an extremely high level of mental, physical, and even emotional energy. That brings me to the sub-title of this chapter. Here's the thing . . .

THiNG # 17

THE ENEMY OF GROWTH IS COMFORT!

There's little that's comfortable in learning to dance. There's little that's comfortable in learning or becoming most things. Becoming a professional of any kind requires tremendous work over a long period of time, taxing the very strongest among us. Being "comfortable" has little to do with learning or becoming anything.

So, if it's so uncomfortable, even to point of great mental and physical strain, how or why does anyone attempt to learn anything? That's where one's talents (natural propensities) mixed with one's passion (burning desire), further mixed with the joy and satisfaction that comes from growth and accomplishment come in to play. (Remember Steven's Saying # 2: "Enjoy your struggle".)

If you can embrace the joy you have in doing what you're naturally gifted to do, and keep that joy in your thinking during the work process, you will be much more apt to avoid discouragement and continue on to your desired goal. As you see your level of understanding as well as your physical capabilities improve, you'll be a first-hand witness to how your investment of hard work has paid off. Your improvement will be the impetus that gives you the incentive to work for even greater achievement.

Take the long way, it's shorter . . .

Now, in terms of the actual work process, contrary to popular belief, there are no real short cuts. The commercials are wrong! There is no special device one can buy that can bring great results with little or no effort. No, it takes mucho grande efforts.

Another one of the many sayings Steven Peck was known for was: **"The long way is the short way, and the short way is the long way!"** (Steven's saying #3).

What that means is, if you spend the time and do the work that's required up front, though it'll take longer than you'd like, it will produce a stronger, more solid, longer-lasting result which will not require revisiting later on. If you try to take short cuts, thereby skipping a few steps in the process, though you may seem to arrive at your destination sooner, the results are tenuous at best.

Exhibits "A", "B" and "C" . . .

I give you the Three Little Pigs as exhibit "A", "B" and "C". Oh sure, the cocky, smart-ass pig (exhibit "A") who built his house out of straw was finished first and was able to play while the others continued working, but was his house strong enough to withstand potential dangers? What about the equally cocky, though slightly less foolish pig (exhibit "B") who built his house out of wood—yes, he showed more foresight than the smart-ass pig but, still, could his house withstand the inevitable tests? No, the only truly smart and wise pig (exhibit "C") took the long way, which in the long run proved to be the short way, and built his house out of brick which was able to withstand anything that could come against it.

Sure he had to work considerably harder and longer, carrying those heavy bricks from the local big box store, mixing the mortar and waiting for each layer to set and dry, but when he was finished, he was finished! He had a solid place he could invite the local chiropractor in to adjust his weary, whacked-out back from all that heavy lifting.

The concept is known as deferred, or *delayed gratification*. Though he took considerably longer to build his house, when it was completed, it offered protection from all the elements, including that nasty, crafty big, bad voodoo daddy wolf. Because of their impatience (childish immaturity), the two cocky pigs found themselves covered in spices with an apple stuffed in their mouths. Moral of the story: The wise pig will put in the time and work up-front knowing that what seems to be the long way is ultimately the short way.

Conclusion . . .

There's one last point I wish to emphasize. It's something that seems to astonish many of my students. **"Growth necessitates change!" (Dennonism #10)** Change doesn't necessarily mean growth, mind you, but growth does necessarily mean change. One of the greatest leaders and orators of the 20th century, Winston Churchill, put it this way: "To improve is to change; to be perfect is to change often."

There are more than a few students of mine each semester who show very little change (meaning improvement) in their work habits over time, and therefore, very little change, (again—meaning improvement), in their capabilities as a result. Simply put—their work habits have not improved sufficiently to improve their dancing. Believe me, it's not their "talent" that's holding them back. It's their work ethic.

It is so important to know and understand the Four Factors that determine one's success in order to fully appreciate what one's responsibility is. With that knowledge and understanding, a person can make the most of a given situation to optimize the likelihood of reaching their "full potential". Once again, they are:

1. **TALENT** – Gifts from God.
2. **PASSION/DESIRE** – The fire that fuels the desire.
3. **EXCELLENT INSTRUCTION** - An absolute must.
4. **WORK ETHIC** – It's all up to you, baby!

Remember, people who are successful at learning anything -- be it artistic, athletic, or academic -- don't rely on, or even expect, luck to play a part. To the extent something happens in life that brings fortune your way, then good for you. But if your plan is to wait on "happenstance" to bring you good fortune, you'll probably be waiting a very long time.

I heard film and TV producer Jerry Bruckheimer, of *Pirates of the Caribbean* and *CSI* fame, being interviewed on television about his enormous success. His take on luck was this: "The harder you work, the luckier you get." There it is—it's all up to you and it's all about the work.

If you're truly interested in learning what goes into making a "strong, personal proactive work ethic" you'll want to read the next couple of chapters. We're going to dig deep to get at the very root cause of "excellence", because it is excellence in one's approach to their work effort -- be it at school, one's place of employment, or in one's personal life -- that leads to great achievement and ultimate success.

CHAPTER SIX
TEN KEYS TO EXCELLENCE
ANATOMY OF AN EXCELLENT WORK ETHIC!

"Every body is lazy!" In the late 1970s, Sayhber was assisting choreographer Ron Poindexter on the *American Music Awards*. Ron was a really terrific guy who truly appreciated her talents. We both had worked for him several times, but during this particular time, I was on the road touring with the Ann-Margret Show so I was unable to be a part of it. Sayhber was hired as both his assistant and performer.

Among the several numbers the dancers were involved in, there was a final number they were to perform while the closing credits would scroll across the screen. The ladies of the dance were wearing these cumbersome dresses that were designed to look elegant but, as is often the case in show business, looks can be deceiving. Because there was no way of knowing how long the scrolling of credits would take, the dance was designed to loop itself over and over again as long as necessary till the signal was given to the musical conductor to close out the music.

Well, the scrolling of credits seemed to take forever and the dancers, like the pros they were, kept going and going, repeatedly looping the dance many times over. The audience members were held captive watching this repetitive, never-ending number, which was rapidly becoming tedious. Sayhber, who only knows one way to perform -- full out -- was right there in the front dancing her little heart out when the top of her dress began to unravel and fall apart.

Long before Janet Jackson's infamous mishap during the 2004 Super Bowl halftime show, Sayhber was at the beginning stages of having her own "wardrobe malfunction". She knew that as long as the music was playing, the cameras were on them and she had to keep going, no matter what. Almost losing her dress entirely, she scooped up the hanging parts and with great panache, she re-doubled her efforts to an even greater height of flamboyancy, transforming what was a rather boring exercise in repetition to an electrified atmosphere of wonderment while all eyes watched in anticipation to see whether or not the dress would last as long as she did.

When the number was finally allowed to end, Television's Barney Miller, Hal Linden, leapt to his feet leading the celebrity-filled audience into what became an enthusiastic standing ovation. Being a Broadway star in his own right, Linden undoubtedly appreciated the tenacity and professionalism that Sayhber was exhibiting. At that moment, she exemplified the excellence that every professional Broadway performer endeavors to embody. Sayhber knew what was expected of her and knew how to deliver. Her training and approach was such that she had a laser-like ability to concentrate, along with a tenacity of purpose and resolve to make it through any and all difficulties to eventual victory.

Those precious, exceptional, excellent few . . .

I've often lamented to myself, and sometimes out loud to my classes, that they'd progress -- we as a class would progress -- ever so much quicker if I didn't have to spend so much time redirecting their energy, showing them how to apply themselves to the work at hand, showing them what they should be looking for, how to look for those things, and reminding them that it is they who bare the bulk of the responsibility for what they learn and how fast they progress.

There have been times when, out of sheer exasperation, I'll stop, take a deep breath and look directly at my students and say: **"I'm a much better teacher than you are a student!"** (Dennonism #11) That's because, at that moment, I'm putting a lot more effort and care into my teaching than they are into their learning. It's moments like these that remind me of how little understanding a significant number of students have of what their responsibility is in the teaching/learning process.

Whenever Sayhber or I do come across a student who demonstrates a keen understanding of what their part in the process is, we can't help but notice, admire, and appreciate them. It's abundantly clear they operate at a level that stands far above the rest. In our ongoing quest to find ways to elevate all of our students, we decided it was necessary to don surgical masks and perform a highly technical, completely metaphorical, exploratory, surgical dissection on *those precious, exceptional, excellent few* that exemplify the very essence of excellence. Our goal was to get at the very root cause of "excellence". Before I reveal our findings, let us first define the word itself.

• • DEFiNiTiON TiME • •

At its very root, the word "excellence" means to excel at something which, according to my dictionary, means to "be exceptionally good or proficient in an activity or subject." It is the quality of being outstanding. That means standing outside of, or above, what is considered normal, or average.

What's so wrong with being average? . . .

Let's now define and discuss "normal" or average. "Normal" or average is the category that the majority of people fit into. What's wrong with average? For starters, it's not exceptional. Let me put it this way, operating on an average level requires only an average effort. For many, operating on an average level requires little or no effort. In other words, they possess just enough inherent skill (that's skill or ability that requires no extra work to obtain) to perform a given task, or accomplish a given assignment as good as most everyone else. They're average without even trying. That's what's wrong right there—their being average required absolutely no work at all.

If one can do, or be, average without putting forth any real effort, and then be satisfied with that, they're being complacent. Being complacent means being content with where one is. If where one is, is already the best one can possibly be, then being content seems understandable . . . though, as I mentioned in Chapter One, the true artist is never really satisfied or content with their current ability or work effort. They're always striving to do and be better.

What I find most distressing about those that seem content with being average, or doing average work, is that it reveals a complete lack of initiative, motivation and drive. Keep in mind I'm not talking about trying to be the best in the world at any one thing. Striving to be the fastest runner, or best dancer, or most acclaimed scientist are fine goals, but what I'm talking about is becoming the best you, you can be. It's about a personal victory by achieving a personal best.

There are marathon races being held throughout the country every year in which the majority of participants understand they have absolutely no chance to win. They actually don't enter to win. They enter for the sole purpose of challenging themselves. Their goal is mainly to complete the race with the hope of beating their previous time. For them, it's about the challenge and subsequent reward of improvement. Complacency is completely counterproductive to achieving that!

We've also found that many people who seem content with being average are actually suffering from the unwarranted belief that they're already operating at a high level—even an excellent level. I hate to be the bearer of bad news, but believing so does not necessarily make it so. There is a real ignorance amongst many as to what makes for excellence.

Excellence 101 . . .

To my knowledge, there's never been any kind of objective barometer by which to measure one's efforts. How does one know if one is operating at an excellent level? There are no "Excellence 101" courses being offered in schools that I'm aware of. Oh sure the general concept is no doubt referenced, but I'm talking about having a deep, thorough study of the qualities and attributes that make for excellence.

That's what this chapter is all about. That's why we put on our doctor's outfits and performed the dissection. I'm not just going to present a lot of theoretical, conjectural, speculative theories. What I'm going to do is reveal the results of an examination we've performed on *those precious, exceptional, excellent few* students who've graced our classrooms over the past umpteen years. We dug deep to find, isolate and examine the qualities and attributes that are common to each.

The results have yielded certain "keys" that can be isolated, understood and purposefully applied to any learning or working situation. As you read, you can determine for yourself whether or not you've been operating at full excellence capacity. Each of the "keys" is an important part of the whole. They interrelate and overlap each other often, as you will see, but they are, nonetheless, each distinct concepts. The Ten Keys To Excellence are:

**1. Focus   2. Purpose   3. Investment   4. Energy   5. Passion
6. Responsibility   7. Intelligence   8. Gratitude   9. Resolve   10. Respect**

Key # 1: FOCUS

It's not surprising that the first thing we noticed while peering deep inside *those precious, exceptional, excellent few* is their strong ability to tune out any and all distractions and zero in on the situation at hand. It's futile for a teacher to spend time trying to impart knowledge and wisdom to students who are not ready to receive. Can you imagine throwing the ball to the catcher whose mind is wandering? Too many students are not ready to catch the "ball" of info/insight/knowledge that is thrown their way.

Each year there is a growing number of students coming into our classes demonstrating an ever-increasing inability to direct their attention. Not only do they not know how to focus very well, they don't even know what it means to focus. They've obviously not been taught and trained by previous teachers that an essential means by which anyone takes control of their learning situation is by directing their full attention on the teacher as well as the task at hand.

To focus means to place something at the center of one's attention. It's next to impossible to hear, understand, receive and retain any instruction or information when one's mind is otherwise occupied. I've found that when someone doesn't hear me, I know it's because he or she is not actively listening and hearing. What they're dong is thinking—usually about something unrelated to what I'm teaching. I put it this way: **"The number one impediment to hearing is thinking!" (Dennonism #12)**

Julian Treasure, chairman of the Sound Agency (a firm that advises worldwide businesses) is also an international speaker and author on the subject of the effects sounds have on people. He takes it a step further and puts it this way: "The ears are made not for hearing, but for listening. Listening is an active skill -- whereas hearing is passive, listening is something we have to work at. It's a relationship with sound and yet it's a skill that none of us are taught". I love that part—"Listening is an active skill".

Too many students do not know how to actively listen. They allow their minds to wander. Listen to what UCLA psychology professor and memory researcher, Russell Poldrack, Ph.D., found out. It was reported on AOL news about a study he did that says normally, when taking in new information, you process it with the part of the brain called the cerebral cortex. He says, ". . . but multitasking greatly reduces learning because people can't attend to the relevant (new) information."

When multitasking (that means doing and/or thinking of two or more things at once) the brain is forced to switch processing to an area of the brain called the striatum, and the information stored there tends to contain fewer important details. If you want to recall the new information later, you need to pay undivided attention to whatever you want to recall later. Hear that, you need to pay undivided attention.

For new information to be received, one's brain needs to be in a state of receptiveness. I ask my class to stop thinking and focus their attention totally on me. I need their radio dial tuned solely and clearly to my frequency, so there aren't competing stations broadcasting in their brains at the same time. It's important to enter a classroom, workplace situation, or conversation, with a pre-determined decision to tune out the irrelevant, non-essential in order to focus in on the relevant essentials.

The concept is very simple—the greater a person's ability to focus, the greater a person's ability to receive and learn. Those who operate in the realm of excellence understand that whether they're in a business meeting, a classroom, or even a simple conversation with a friend, the only thing that exists at that moment is what is happening right then and there. Key # 1: FOCUS!

Key # 2: PURPOSE

All too often, students dance by habit or rote. Personally, I believe personal habits, like bathing, brushing your teeth, and tipping your instructor after a particularly grueling class are all good, but in the world of dance, habits can actually be harmful. Harmful?

Aren't there good habits as well as bad habits? In the realm of one's personal life, yes, but I have found that when one is taking a dance class, or at an audition, or involved in a rehearsal, dancing by habit means you have no real idea of what you're doing. Here's the thing . . .

THiNG # 18

ALL HABiTS ARE BAD HABiTS!

A dance habit is a reliance on what one has become accustomed to doing, which is generally an unconscious imitation of one's primary teacher. If you're dancing by habit, you're not really noticing how the teacher/choreographer you're currently working with/for wants you to dance . . . and that's bad!

Everything one does in a dance-related situation (any work-related situation) should be done on purpose, with a purpose, for a purpose, toward a purpose. Let me explain it this way.

On purpose:	Consciously—not by habit, routine or rote.
With a purpose:	To do one's best.
For a purpose:	To understand, assimilate and actuate a specific skill/technique.
Toward a purpose:	To be a professional anything, obtaining a college degree, etc.

I know . . . that's a lot of purposes. That's how I teach. I like repetition and redundancy for the purpose of forever searing a point into one's brain. Every aspect of one's work, be it in class, on the job, or in one's personal life should be done *on, with, for* and *toward* a purpose. Habit is the antithesis of purpose.

The lack of purpose in a student's efforts becomes evident when confronted with a new teacher, or when at an audition for a choreographer they've never met before and, no matter what is given or asked for, they dance like they've always danced—the way they're habitually accustomed to. Remember the infamous line: "Now do it like that!" directed to me by my good buddy, Broadway Guy, Ron Field? I was guilty of dancing by habit and that's not a smart thing. I wasn't being observant enough to see that the way the choreographer wanted me to dance and the way I was dancing were two totally different things.

The same principle could be applied to any and all workplace environments. It's not good, or smart, when working for one person to perform one's duties the way a previous employer wanted you to, unless of course the way the new employer wants you to work is the same.

One of the things I endeavor to teach and train my classes to do is to use their eyes and see the differences. Whether overt or subtle, differences are differences and need to be noticed. That's the challenge for anyone who steps into a new situation, be it a class, an audition, or rehearsal—to see the differences.

True story time . . .

Once upon a time there was a young, shy, very naive dancer who went to her first audition for a T.V. show. The show was *The Carol Burnett Show*, which became a wildly successful variety show on CBS from 1967 to 1978. The choreographer was Ernie Flatt, and his assistant was Carlton Johnson.

It seems there was this 15-year old young lady who had been taking dance classes from Johnson. Johnson was so taken by her dynamic intensity, as well as her remarkable musicality, that he invited a couple of her older friends to attend an audition he was going to hold for the upcoming Burnett Show, and to please bring the kid. Though the kid was an experienced performer, she was clearly too young to actually get the job. It turned out to be the usual "cattle call" with dozens of young women, all decked out in their sexy outfits, complete with heels.

The kid had no real experience of how things worked at a professional audition, which was evidenced by her basic classroom dance attire, which consisted of a simple black leotard, black tights, and the very popular (at the time) white sneakers. Johnson proceeded to teach the Ernie Flatt routine and, as is usually the case, broke the dancers into groups to show their "stuff". Midway through the audition, Johnson unexpectedly told everyone to clear the floor. He then asked the kid to step out on the floor and perform the number all by herself, solo, with no one else . . . just her. Too nervous to object, she proceeded to dance as best she could with all the energy and vigor she knew how. After her performance, Johnson proceeded to tell all the other women that that was how he wanted them to do it.

This young thing, who had never met, or even heard of Ernie Flatt before, somehow managed to do his work in such a way as to become the example of how all these older, experienced pros should do it. The kid must have been pretty good, huh? Good, yes, but more importantly, she was very observant, or dare I say, smart? She purposed to demonstrate her ability to capture the style and nuances of what the choreographer wanted.

This story points out the frustration that choreographers and teachers all over the world share. That is, no matter what is demonstrated and/or asked for, many invariably end up dancing the way they've always danced, completely ignoring the intent of the teacher/choreographer.

As I said in the Preface, the dancer's job is to make the choreographer's work, work, and you're not going to make it work if you're dancing one person's dance using somebody else's style/technique/way! Oh, by the way, the 15-year-old kid was none other than my future partner in life, the ever-so-observant Sayhber Rawles. Key # 2: PURPOSE!

Key # 3: INVESTMENT

The next thing we find in our high achievers is an understanding of the concept of "investment". Investment is what one does for the purpose of gaining a profit. *Those precious, exceptional, excellent few* have a willingness to put in the time, effort and work up front, in order to reap the benefits later. They understand the concept of delayed gratification. (Remember those smart-ass pigs?) They see the work not as a punitive, tedious, time-consuming chore that has been imposed on them in order to keep them from enjoying life, but rather as an investment for which they are the beneficiaries. Here's the point: When one thinks of work as an investment rather than expenditure, it can't help but to change one's perspective. This doesn't necessarily make the work easier mind you; it just gives incentive to do the work well, understanding it is the only way to achieve good results.

Those who understand investment have a "bigger picture" view of things. They don't easily get caught up in a moment of self-indulgence. This concept is known as "impulse control". They have the ability to evaluate the long-term repercussions of what they're contemplating doing. They actually think beyond the moment to see if what they're about to do, and how they're about to do it, will reap benefits or detriments.

I'm not saying everything one does needs to be solely about the future. I'm all for having fun moments, or relaxing moments, or completely wild and crazy moments. Those moments can be quite beneficial. They have their time and place, but without looking down the road, "moments" can also get you into trouble. Check out the high school dropout rates, the out-of-wedlock teen pregnancy rates, as well as the enormous amount of credit card debt incurred by many who did not bother to look beyond the "moment".

Toward the end of each semester, when it's already getting too late, there are many students who awaken to the fact that their grade might be in jeopardy. What were they doing the previous three months? They certainly weren't overly concerned with doing whatever was needed in order to get an "A", let alone to learn anything. Those who operate in the realm of excellence have a wise, mature understanding that what one does at any given moment will have consequences (beneficial or detrimental) that will have to be dealt with sooner or later. I purposely invest my all into every class I teach. Unfortunately, I have found that most students do not. To the extent many students do learn, it's because of the worthy efforts of their instructors. This realization led me to this: **"Most students learn in spite of themselves, not because of themselves!" (Dennonism #13)** Here's the thing . . .

THiNG # 19

THE MATHEMATiCAL EQUATiON FOR OPTiMAL LEARNiNG iS: 100%/100%!

The optimum condition in any learning situation is to have the instructor's full throttle effort matched by the students. If you have an instructor who puts his or her all into the process and a student who does the same, you create a nuclear size explosion of learning/productivity.

In order to alleviate my own frustrations, and save my sanity (not to mention keep my therapist's bill to a minimum), I had to come to the realization and fully accept that, though it is my natural inclination to do so, ultimately: **"I cannot care more about my student's progress than they do!" (Dennonism #14)**

So, that's exactly what I've endeavored to do over the years . . . to get my students to care more. That's a major part of why I'm writing this book. I've found it absolutely necessary to drill into my students that they must make a conscious decision on how much of themselves they are going to invest. Then the amount they decide upon will be matched by me. If they want more of me (meaning my knowledge, expertise, and time) they must invest more of themselves. Key # 3: INVESTMENT!

Key # 4: ENERGY

As we continue our examination of those who clearly stand above the rest, we find an extraordinarily high content of self-generated energy. Energy refers to the strength and vitality that's needed to sustain a physical or mental activity. What's important to know is the energy that's used by those who operate at an exceptional level is self-generated.

There are a substantial number of students enrolled in my class at any given time (therefore, I surmise, who are enrolled in anyone's class) who look to and wait for me, or their fellow students, or a lightning bolt, or possibly the transporter room on the Starship Enterprise to energize them. Their battery always seems to be low, so they rely on some force outside of themselves for the energy that they themselves cannot, or will not, generate. These students fall into the category of "energy-sucking leeches". If left unchecked they'll suck the life right out of anyone and everyone around them including the very room itself!

My experience has taught me that these people have no idea how much of a drain they are to their teachers and fellow classmates. The same, I'm sure, applies to any workplace. The ability to excel depends on the person bringing and using his or her own energy source.

I can tell you that continually putting out an enormous amount of energy does not come easily. That's because -- listen closely, for this is extremely important: **"Every body is lazy!" (Dennonism #15)** Not every person, mind you, just every "body". The battle to be energetic and purposeful in one's training is not between a person and some outside force. The battle is between the person, period . . . or should I say exclamation point!

Every body would just as soon be sitting down, or lying down with their favorite beverage in one hand and the T.V. remote in the other and a slice of pizza in the other (I know, too many hands), watching some mindless show that requires no real effort -- meaning energy -- on their part to comprehend. That's what the "body" wants to do. It's up to the person inside, to win the battle against his or her own laziness by being determined to put forth the necessary energy to learn/achieve/grow.

That's what *those precious, exceptional, excellent few* do. Whether they feel like it or not, they start up their own generators, rev up their engines, and proceed to make and use their own energy. They are contributors to their learning or working environment. They add life (meaning energy) to the proceedings. They're the kind of person -- the energetic person -- that others want to be around. Key # 4: ENERGY!

Key # 5: PASSION

Adjacent to the energy quality we find it's sibling, passion. I define passion as energy directed. It's an enormous amount of enthusiasm -- an almost uncontrollable feeling -- directed toward a specific purpose or end. Though this quality is related to energy, it actually takes on a stronger intensity, as it is directed toward a destination such as acquired knowledge, learned skill, or completed task.

Because most people are passive to the point of waiting on their feelings to stimulate them to action, their efforts are all too often halfhearted. So what's a person to do—you either have passion for something or you don't, right? Well, yes and no. First and foremost, passionate people are people whose passion is generated from an enormous desire to succeed.

Having a desire to succeed is a result of how and what one thinks. That's why good parents try to instill confidence in their young by regurgitating the oft-used adage, "You can be anything you want", which is usually followed up, and correctly so, with "if you work hard enough". Though it may be a stretch to actually become anything you want, even if you work hard, it's for sure you won't become anything at all if you don't work hard. What's important is the general sense of hope and expectation. Everybody needs to believe that they can improve upon their present situation.

What we found in our examination of *those precious, exceptional, excellent few* is a mindset (that's a pre-established set of attitudes) that fosters a desire (an outgrowth of how one thinks) to grow and achieve. The truth is, a person's thinking can either help or hinder growth and achievement. Whatever one's social or economic status in life, the right kind of thinking will help create a mindset that in turn directs one's energy toward accomplishment. Can you say Oprah Winfrey?

So what is the right kind of thinking? I say it's thinking that one has control over one's own learning, growth, achievement and, yes, overall life. In other words, one's improvement or achievements are a result of one's own work effort. There's no need for, and one shouldn't wait for, someone else to do something.

What's important here is to understand that a person's mindset dictates one's thinking, which in turn influences one's efforts or actions. The right kind of thinking can actually generate passion, and that passion can in turn produce a work effort that brings about a desired result. Sounds like some kind of mystical, metaphysical mumbo jumbo, but it's not. It's just how the mind works. Believe you have the ability to affect change, and you'll be more likely to put in the necessary work to do so. It's the work that does the changing, and it's the thinking that produces the work.

Changing your thinking changes your perspective, which will indeed change your efforts. *Those precious, exceptional, excellent few* not only believe they have a right to become whatever it is they want to be; they understand it is up to them to supply the directed energy, i.e. passion, to do so. Passion comes from a mindset that demonstrates a purposeful desire and determination to do all one can do in order to get the most out of any given situation. Key # 5: PASSION!

Key # 6: RESPONSIBILITY

As we probe deeper, we find something that I believe is sorely lacking in just about every aspect of today's society. *Those precious, exceptional, excellent few* do something that most do not—they take responsibility for both their successes and, get this now, their failures! No matter what happens, their first tendency is to point the finger of blame, not to some outside person or force, but toward themselves. That means if they're not achieving all of what they'd like to, they'll first explore the probability that they themselves aren't doing all they could. They do not see themselves as the victim of a situation for which they have no control. They see themselves as smart, able-bodied victors, who could do more!

Again, it's a mindset that says no matter how difficult a situation may seem, there is something, or many somethings they could do to better their situation. They understand that whether or not their instructor, or boss, or even parent does all of what the student or worker or teen thinks they should, it is still incumbent upon them to do all of what they can and, if necessary, more. That means if the instructor or workplace manager is somewhat lax in their duties, the responsible student or worker will pick up the slack.

"You mean I should do my teacher's or manager's job?" No, not really. What I mean is if you're really determined to achieve, no matter what the obstacles are, you'll be willing to do whatever extra work that may be needed and spend whatever extra time is necessary, knowing it ultimately all works out to your benefit.

Yes, it can be very difficult, discouraging and just plain agonizing when one is saddled with a teacher, or boss, or even a parent whose abilities to lead, teach or manage, let alone inspire, is less than stellar. Unfortunately, there are those who operate in these positions who ought not be there, but they are and, unless we're able to change our circumstance to find a better teacher, or boss, or parent, we have to deal with them. *Those precious, exceptional, excellent few* are a determined lot who will do their Lewis and Clark thing, turn on their inner GPS system, and search out the best possible route to victory.

I mentioned grades earlier. Toward the middle of each semester I take the opportunity to discuss the real meaning of their year-end grade. Many are hoping to matriculate to a University and they'll be required to forward their transcripts. I ask them, what do their grades reveal about them? Should a potential employer request their transcripts, what is he or she trying to determine? "It represents how smart I am" and "It shows how hard I worked" are the two answers most given. They're both true, but there's another way to look at it that might help one to understand why it's imperative to always do one's best. Here's the thing . . .

THiNG # 20

YOUR GRADE REPRESENTS YOUR ABiLiTY TO NAViGATE AND NEGOTiATE YOUR WAY THROUGH A GiVEN SYSTEM!

Just as sailors must have the ability to navigate the seas to successfully complete a voyage, so must a student/worker. One's grade reveals a person's ability to figure out what's required of him or her from a particular teacher/boss for a particular class or workplace environment.

It's a different kind of "smarts" that goes beyond book learning. The ability to determine what's needed represents a level of shrewdness and savviness that's attractive to any prospective school or employer.

Responsible students and workers will begin sizing up their instructors and bosses the very first day they meet them. They understand each teacher or boss is different, so the requirements will be different. Because the oceans of each situation are different, savvy students and workers understand the importance of not assuming for a minute that what any previous person of authority required of him or her would be the same as any current person of authority.

At some point during the first few meetings of any class I teach, I'll have the students look directly at me. I tell them that there is one person in this class whom they need to figure out and be responsible to, and that's me. I'm not one of their previous teachers, and I'm also not going to become 30 or 50 different personalities to accommodate all of them.

I'm going to be me, and it's up to them to figure out what I want and work to that. That's their responsibility—that's their job. It is my opinion that students are being coddled more and more these days, and their ability to work through average situations, let alone difficult situations, are quite limited. I'll be talking directly to and about instructors in Act Three, but right now I'll just say that we teachers (not to mention we parents) do our students a disservice by babying them. Here's the thing . . .

THiNG # 21

By insisting my students take full responsibility for what and how much they learn, what I'm really doing is challenging their thinking, or lack thereof, in hopes that they may begin to understand that their status quo, lackadaisical, apathetic approach to learning is keeping them from growing up and maturing into the very best they can be, and that the dance class they're taking from me is more than just a "fun" non-essential class.

The dance class, like all classes regardless of subject matter, represents yet another opportunity for them to practice (which is what it takes) taking charge of their learning. It is yet another opportunity (which life is ever so full of) for them to overcome challenges (which is what achievement is all about) by putting their very best effort forward in a persistent, consistent manner so they can prove to themselves and everyone else that they are a capable, responsible and mature learner.

You see, it's not just the actual subject matter that's important. It's the ability to learn the subject matter, for a good student is a good student no matter what the subject is. That brings me to another one of Mr. Peck's insightful sayings: **"How you are in dance is how you are in life, and how you are in life is how you are in dance!" (Steven's saying #4)**

Your character traits are not just revealed in your dance classes. They're revealed in every class. Let's face it, they're revealed in every situation. You're not a different person when you dance—you're always you. You're not a different person in your math class than you are anywhere else. Yes, you may have a greater aptitude for one subject over another, but you're either resourceful, creative and capable, or you're not.

The grade you receive at the end of the semester (even for such non-academic courses as dance) reveals as much about your understanding of the concept of hard work, creativity, and just plain bull-dogged tenacity, i.e. responsibility, double i.e. adulthood, as it does on how much knowledge you may have acquired. So, next time you think your final grades don't really matter—think again. Key # 6: RESPONSIBILITY!

Key # 7: INTELLIGENCE

Wouldn't you know that as we continue on with our examination, we find something like intelligence? The concept of intelligence has to do with both actual intelligence and the perception of intelligence. Believe it or not, they both reflect and affect each other.

Let's start with perception. It's unfortunate, but most people are completely unaware of their demeanor, what it projects to others, and how it affects their learning. I've seen many a student (actually all kinds of people) who, by their outward appearance, seem to be somewhat dimwitted, only to find out later that they're much smarter than they look. *Those precious, exceptional, excellent few* understand that their physical stance (which includes posture, facial expression, as well as overall attitude) projects a "look" for which others will (not maybe, or possibly, but will) determine his or her involvement, level of concentration and yes, overall intelligence. Whether it's fair or not, a book can't help but be judged by the cover, at least at first.

Marketing people spend an enormous amount of time and money deciding on the "perfect" book cover, knowing it could make or break its success. They know that if the book is going to sell, the potential reader first needs to be attracted to it. That means they need to be enticed to walk over and pick it up. Packaging is a very important aspect of marketing anything, and those who traverse the roads of excellence understand this. I don't wish to alarm anyone, but every person is in a perpetual state of self-marketing whether they know it or not. That means you're being judged at all times. Being judged? How offensive! Well it's the truth but, if you like, I can use a kinder, gentler word—how about "evaluated"? Either which way, it still means someone is looking at you for the purpose of making a decision about you, which could ultimately affect your present and future. It is only through "evaluations" that jobs are attained and promotions achieved.

One of the least politically correct people I've ever known, you guessed it, Mr. Steven Peck, had a direct, cutting way of calling our attention to our "look". If he sensed we weren't as focused on him and what he was saying as he'd like, he'd stop and blurt out: **"Don't look stupid!" (Steven's saying #5)** He had us work on our stance, our facial expressions, and most certainly, our overall attitude, in order to achieve a more involved, purposeful, "intelligent" look. It all comes down to body language.

Long before anyone gets to know you, you are judged—sorry, evaluated—by what your body and face are saying. Most people don't realize that before they ever get a chance to open their mouth to prove how "smart" they believe they are, it may be too late because their body or face has already spoken. In fact, it's been screaming! That's why it's important to be concerned with one's "look".

Please understand, Mr. Peck was not saying we were stupid. He was saying we looked stupid! There's a big difference. As I ask my students: "Who's your friend, the one who passes by and stares, or the one who actually stops and tells you your fly is open?"

There are many very bright individuals who allow themselves to have an outward look that projects unintelligence. Why? The reason is simple; they've never ever thought about what their appearance might project. No one has ever bothered to educate them as to how they can put their best demeanor forward with a purposeful, intelligent look. Steven Peck didn't like talking to a group of students who, knowingly or not, looked disinterested or as he put it, stupid. Me either. That was many years ago and, ever since, both Sayhber and I do our best to teach our students how to project an engaged, intelligent look.

Shouldn't individuals be judged on their actual intelligence? In a perfect, clairvoyant world, yes, but as the saying goes . . . perception is reality. (Remember Thing # 2: It's not good enough to be good. You need to be smart!) Well, here's the thing . . .

THiNG # 22

IT'S NOT GOOD ENOUGH TO BE SMART, YOU NEED TO LOOK SMART!

The effort to project intelligence is really an effort to project involvement, which serves to center or focus one's attention. Like any picture, the visual image your body, and face, projects speaks volumes. You may never be considered for a position, or a promotion, if you are perceived to be uninterested or "dimwitted".

It's an important truth I started with, so I'll say it again—most people are completely unaware of their "look", what it projects to others and how that ultimately affects them. A person who is concerned with his or her "image" (as it relates to "smarts") will more likely be fully engaged, actively listening, participating, and ready and able to receive.

Here's the kicker—while endeavoring to look smart, the student is actually engaged in the process of becoming smart. Curious, huh? Our mothers were right when they nagged us to sit up straight and pay attention. Mom knew that a slumping posture, along with the unfocused, uninvolved expression on our faces served to repel any and all incoming information . . . like the Starship Enterprise when it puts up its force fields to fend off incoming missiles. Those that work in the realm of excellence are acutely aware of both their actual and perceived intelligence. Key # 7: INTELLIGENCE!

Key # 8: GRATITUDE

As we probe even deeper into *those precious, exceptional, excellent few*, we find this lovely, refreshing sense of appreciation. It's an attitude based on an understanding of a rather simple, but oh so very important concept: That which is not appreciated is not valued; and, that which is not valued is not appreciated! Either which way you put it, the very act of being grateful has an influence on how one approaches one's work.

Being grateful means giving recognition or credit to a source that has done or is doing something we find beneficial. The source could be a teacher, a boss, an institution, or a workplace. It could also be the very subject matter we're learning. What's important to understand is that the level of one's appreciation for something reveals the value, usefulness and significance that one places on that something. If one has little or no appreciation, that means they see little or no value or usefulness for what it is they are doing. How can one learn something he or she has little regard for?

I always hear from young ones (and not so young ones) that they don't find what they're learning or doing particularly relevant to their lives. "It's not relevant" is code for "boring". Once again, I'll be addressing the instructors in Act Three on this and many other issues, but right now I'm most concerned with the general understanding of the importance of gratitude. Whether a particular subject is perceived as boring or not, what's clear from our examination is *those precious, exceptional, excellent few* have a basic appreciation for the general concept of learning. They want to learn. Sure, they have areas of study they find more enticing than others, but at the very core of their being is a gratefulness for the opportunity to learn, grow and achieve.

What are they, some kind of weirdo? Absolutely. They belong to the minority of people who look beyond the moment and understand that it is they who are the beneficiaries of all the work they put in. By definition, they are weird, or strange or peculiar—in other words, exceptional!

At some point everyone needs to make an important decision. Do you want to be among the mortal masses and be average, or do you want to be counted among the precious few and be excellent? If it's excellent you want to be, then you'll begin to appreciate all things concerned with the educational/work process. Key # 8: GRATITUDE!

Key # 9: RESOLVE

The next thing we find in our exploration is something that is absolutely essential to the concept of excellence. Unlike most people's New Year's resolutions, which often go unfulfilled, a resolve is a "quality decision" to see something through no matter what. To resolve to do something is not just a desire or hope to do something. It is an absolute commitment to oneself to see a desired result come to fruition.

We've found that those who operate in the realm of excellence understand that before they can accomplish anything they must decide on exactly what they want, how far they're willing to go, and how hard they're willing to work to obtain it. One might think that the concept of doing one's best is a no-brainer, but without making a conscious, deliberate decision to do so, and then following it up with the requisite work (yes, it's always about work), one will most likely not see the desired results.

I want to address the response we get most often when chastising someone for less than stellar work—"I'm trying". The resolve I'm talking about is one that says: "I'm willing to do what it takes for as long as it takes". That's resolve. It's pretty much the antithesis of "trying" . . . at least the way most people understand it.

I know that parents, teachers, and managers all over the world often tell their charges to "try to do your best—that's all I ask". The problem with the word "try" is that it's too often used as a "get out of jail free" card, meaning if one falls short of the desired goal, they're to be forgiven or excused because, after all, they "tried". Trying usually means a person will put a nominal amount of effort into something and if they don't see immediate results they'll get discouraged and stop. They then can say they "tried", but it just wasn't meant to be. Simply put, the mindset of trying allows for defeat.

Those who succeed don't entertain the thought of failure as it pertains to their personal achievements. That doesn't mean they never fail at anything -- not at all -- it just means they keep their thoughts and energies directed on the goal they've set before them. It also means they don't see their so-called failures as reasons to quit. Failure merely represents an annoying, temporary setback that serves to energize them to re-examine their approach, make the necessary changes, and then re-double their efforts.

Barely a war in history has been won without failures (battle losses), but that doesn't mean one should give up. If that were the case, there'd be no U.S. of A. During the first year of World War II we lost so many battles that a mindset of giving up would have left us all speaking German or Japanese. My point is that when one resolves to do something, accomplish something, or learn something, there will be temporary setbacks, for sure, but that need not lead to ultimate failure.

An important point to note here is that goals need to be realistic. Great achievers don't achieve great destinations overnight. It's always one step at a time. The inventors of airplanes didn't set unrealistic goals like flying to the moon, not at first anyway.

The Wright Bothers counted themselves successful when their first flight took them a whopping 20 feet off the ground for all of 12 seconds. Because of their resolve, over time, and with continual great effort, their flights continually improved. The point is that one's ultimate goal, be it becoming a professional dancer, singer, writer, businessperson, doctor, lawyer, or college graduate, is reached through reasonable, feasible increments.

Open up your brain now because what I'm about to say is vitally important. Becoming something in the future requires becoming an excellent worker in the present. That means doing the work that is presently set before you in the most excellent way possible. (Remember the one truly smart pig?) That's how victory is achieved. Becoming an excellent worker requires a quality decision and commitment. If that decision is a strong resolve (remember—willing to do whatever it takes for as long as it takes) then success can't help but be achieved. Key # 9: RESOLVE!

Key # 10: RESPECT

The final thing we discover, as we complete our probe into *those precious, exceptional, excellent few*, is something that gets to the very core of everything we've discussed thus far. Every person we've examined who operates at a high level of excellence has this one quality that serves as the very foundation of how they operate.

Respect is what one demonstrates when one has a deep admiration for someone or something. That's important—"a deep admiration". Students must understand that the level of respect they have for all things concerned with education, work, and life itself, has a profound affect on his or her ability to learn, achieve and grow. Being respectful means being open, which is the state of mind in which one must operate in order to receive. In other words: no respect—no learning.

There are several aspects of "respect" to highlight. Let me first start with an admiration for the very concept of learning itself. Learning is a good thing! **"There is nothing you'll ever learn that you will not use, someway, somehow, somewhere!" (Dennonism #16)** That's something I've said countless times to my children as well as in my classes. It's not always received well, but it still was and is my responsibility as my children's father and my students' instructor to impact their thinking.

It doesn't matter whether it's dance, music, athletics, math, science, history, or any other course. Every subject matter deserves respect, whether one has an affinity for it or not. Every one of these disciplines has been explored, experimented with and developed over hundreds, if not thousands, of years for the benefit of humanity. Even if you believe the subject matter to be completely irrelevant and so very uninteresting, remember: at the very least you're broadening your knowledge base, exercising your learning skills, and don't forget what I said before—no information or skill one learns will go unused!

If nothing else, you'll be able to hold your own in a conversation about a variety of subjects with anyone, anytime, anywhere. What's wrong with that? You might even be considered the "smart" one at the party and, who knows, it may lead to a job offer, a promotion, or quite possibly a really hot date! You may even get the opportunity to win tens of thousands of dollars on a game show. Just ask the folks who've appeared on *Jeopardy*.

In addition to respecting any given subject matter, one must have a respect for the very institutions where that learning occurs. The schools, colleges, universities, dance studios, and any and all other learning institutions deserve respect because they're there for the betterment of the individual as well as the whole of society. The very buildings themselves are in one sense "holy" or set apart institutions that deserve a certain reverence. I'm appalled by the disrespectful treatment that many of the buildings, walkways, hallways, and even parking lots receive from students who've clearly not been educated on the benefits of an attitude of respect. Key #10: RESPECT!

True stroy time . . .

Some time ago, a professor was making his way to the parking lot at one of the colleges where he taught. As he came close to his car he noticed that a young lady -- she appeared to be 18 or 19 -- was just starting up her cute little sports car (no doubt a gift from Daddy). As he came closer to his car he noticed her placing her fast food trash on the ground next to her car. He thought, just maybe, with him only a few feet away from her that she'd be a bit embarrassed by her blatant disregard and disrespect of the school parking lot. No, not at all. Before she took off, the professor spoke up and said: "You're not going to do that, are you?" She looked at him defiantly as if to say he had no right to speak to her that way, started up her car and screeched away. You may have guessed that the professor was none other than me, and I wish I could say that this kind of thing happens seldom, but that'd be untrue.

Those who sit, stand, or dance in the office of instructor also deserve respect. I realize that some may find it difficult to respect a teacher before you get to know him or her, but please understand that the respect one demonstrates toward a teacher (actually anyone in a position of authority) they've yet to get to know, or maybe do know but don't particularly like, is really for the position or office which that person occupies.

Believe me, I know from first-hand experience that there are people in positions of authority who, through their actions and behaviors, would seem to deserve little or no respect. Regretably we have to deal with them. If one cannot change his or her circumstances to avoid such a person, then it's best to continue to offer respect for the position if not the person. It is unfortunate, but they hold your grade, or job, in their hands.

Before you get too down on any particular teacher, here's something you may not have thought of. Everybody becomes a teacher at some point, including you. While some become teachers as a profession, others do so as a by-product of their job. Supervisors, managers, and bosses of all kinds will by necessity become a teacher. A parent, by definition, is a teacher for at least eighteen years—but most parents know it never really ends. At some point, you will find yourself teaching somebody something, so start thinking about how you'd like to be treated.

Respect is an absolutely essential quality to operate in and possess in order to become a successful achiever. It might be helpful to think of it this way—the opposite of respect is contempt. Contempt is believing something is beneath a person or unworthy of their consideration. I ask you, how can one learn if one has contempt? Respect for the concept of education, respect for the institutions that offer the education, respect for the subject matter one is studying, and respect for the instructor are extremely important and essential if one is to rise above the "norm".

Warning - No esteem ahead!

There's one other, very important aspect of respect that has to do with self. The concept of self-respect has been hijacked and distorted in my opinion. I'm about to go way off the deep end here, so take a moment, look around, and find something to grab hold of—you may want to hit me with it later. I believe one of the major reasons we have so many showing so little respect (self or otherwise) in this day and age can be attributed to the well-intentioned, but totally misguided, movement called "self-esteem". Before you swing at me with whatever you grabbed hold of, please hear me out.

Esteem versus respect - the battle of the ages . . .

Unlike previous generations, for the past couple of decades, young ones have been taught to "esteem" themselves for no other reason than they exist. "I am, therefore I must be great". They've been taught to think quite highly of themselves for no other reason . . . than they were born (as if they had anything to do with that).

Sounds innocent enough. Isn't it good for a child to grow up believing they're worthy of everyone's esteem—especially their own? Well . . . I vote no. Don't hit me just yet. Unless a person's esteem is based on a well-founded, well-grounded foundation of having been earned, a person's esteem is valueless. That's the problem with today's incessant obsession with self-esteem—it hasn't been earned!

If one is taught to think real highly of oneself for no other reason than they exist, then where does the most important motivator we have in life called "incentive" come from? Where's the incentive to work hard, or to develop one's skills come from? Where's the incentive to achieve? Where's the incentive to do anything except those things that would be considered easy or "fun", and even those things lose their fun factor sooner or later, so then where's the incentive to continue or complete anything? It's missing because there is no need. After all, if you already think you're a great person, what's the point?

Incentive is at the heart of any thing, any goal, any objective, any prize, or any position desired. It's what motivates, encourages, and stimulates us to be industrious and work our very hardest. I believe that with the advent of the "self-esteem" movement, the incentive to work hard or develop one's skills, or to achieve anything has greatly diminished. In our collective 80-plus years of teaching we continually come across students who, by everything they say and do, demonstrate how very highly they think of themselves, yet prove time and again to be lazy, unfocused, and completely unmotivated.

I've been mulling this over for many years now and believe I have come up with what I believe to be a far better term to use. It's nothing new mind you, but instead of "esteem", we'd be far better served if we brought back that good 'ol stand-by term—that of "respect".

You may think I'm making another distinction without a difference, but I believe there is a difference and that difference is profoundly important. Here's the difference: whereas self-esteem is something everyone is taught to have regardless of whether they do, earn or achieve anything, respect is something that is bestowed upon those we admire for what they have done, whether it be athletic, artistic, or academic.

There are performers we admire for their amazing abilities to sing and entertain us—Sinatra, Garland, Streisand, Caruso, Domingo, etc. There are musicians whose virtuosity is beyond human—Yo Yo Ma, Louis Armstrong, Carlos Santana, etc. There are sports stars whose athletic skills truly astound us—Serena Williams, Babe Ruth, Michael Phelps, etc. There are beautiful dancers whose skills and artistry bring about a sense of awe and wonderment—Astaire, Hines, Baryshnikov, etc.

There are those in the world of finance and business who build great empires and make gazillions of dollars because of talents and highly-developed skills the rest of us only dream of. There are those who have a great ability to mentor, instruct and motivate. (You'll read more about them in Act Three when I zero in on teachers.) What do all these people have in common? Through dedication, commitment and hard, hard work, they have achieved a level of success in their fields that the rest of us can't help but admire and, yes, respect.

That's why I'm against what are called "participation trophies". You know—where everyone gets a trophy just because they showed up. It's all part of the self-esteem movement which teaches that everyone is a "winner". Well, it's simply not true and we do our young ones a disservice by not teaching them that achievement is earned, not bestowed. That's vitally important so I'll say it again: "Acheivment is **EARNED**, not bestowed!"

There are many lessons that can only be learned in "failure", the most important of which is that one need not be defeated in defeat. Not giving up is lesson number one—in other words, tenacity. Understanding that it is not the end of the world if one doesn't "win" on any particular day, as long as he or she learns how to regroup and rethink their strategy as well as redouble their energy toward an eventual victory.

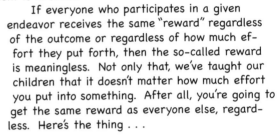

Keep in mind, winners are not people who never fail. They're simply people who don't give up! A momentary defeat is really an opportunity to assess one's approach and strategy to see if an adjustment is in order.

If everyone who participates in a given endeavor receives the same "reward" regardless of the outcome or regardless of how much effort they put forth, then the so-called reward is meaningless. Not only that, we've taught our children that it doesn't matter how much effort you put into something. After all, you're going to get the same reward as everyone else, regardless. Here's the thing . . .

THiNG # 23

THiNGS EARNED ARE THiNGS APPRECiATED ARE THiNGS RESPECTED!

When someone truly earns their success, advancement, or reward -- knowing the amount of work it required doing so -- they gain a greater appreciation for that advancement, or reward. Their appreciation translates into a greater **respect** for all things concerned, especially themselves.

Simply put, the true value of something is based on what one has to do to earn it. If one is simply given something for just being there, it obviously wasn't earned and therefore has no real value. It's basically worthless. Attics, basements and closets all over America are full of unearned, unvalued trophies.

In 1776, Thomas Paine wrote in his book *Common Sense* that: "What we obtain too cheap we esteem too lightly; it is dearness only that gives everything its value". He wasn't just talking about independence from Great Britain. Generally, what makes something "dear" is the work one has to do in order to acheive that something. That's what gives it its value—true value.

When one accomplishes a task, a job, or is awarded a promotion of some kind because they worked very hard over a considerable period of time, then one has a compelling reason to respect oneself—and for that they have a real reason, an "earned" reason, to "feel" good about themself. Notice I put respect before feelings. Earned respect trumps any conjured up self-esteem a person has been told he or she should have just for being alive.

The joy one experiences after having learned, earned or achieved something by employing an excellent work ethic cannot be matched by anything in this world. It's what I call an: **"Achievement high!" (Dennonism #17)** It's far superior to any drug-induced high (not that I have any first-hand experience). It's an inner thrill that one really does deserve, for it is born out of accomplishment, not just existence.

The "high" of achievement serves to encourage and motivate a person to do still more things so they may experience that thrill again. Ultimately, it's not the trophy, the black belt, or certificate of graduation, or even the money we earn that's the most important thing . . . it's the actual sense of accomplishment or achievement that's the real reward.

What better "feeling" to have about oneself than that of "respect" because of something you've earned or accomplished. It need not be something monumental or earth shattering, either. It might just be a well-prepared report you did for one of your classes. It could be for an exceptional, excellent effort you put forth in one of your dance classes. It could be for any job that was well done—be it at home, school or work. It might be because you helped someone with something they themselves were having trouble with, or you showed kindness to someone at a time when they really needed it. All of these have to do with the concept of "doing", and nothing with the concept of "being". Esteeming oneself highly just because one exists seems counterproductive and, just plain silly to me.

The next time you hear someone talking about the importance of having high self-esteem, think about my argument to replace the word esteem with respect and see if it doesn't make a lot more sense. Now I ask you, do you still want to hit me? Once again, Key # 10: Respect!

Conclusion . . .

We've reached the end of our surgical procedure. Our dissection has revealed ten qualities, or "keys" that are common to all those who operate in the realm of excellence. Once again they are:

1. **Focus**   2. **Purpose**   3. **Investment**   4. **Energy**   5. **Passion**
6. **Responsibility**   7. **Intelligence**   8. **Gratitude**   9. **Resolve**   10. **Respect**

Each key makes up a part of the proverbial excellent work ethic. Now, when someone encourages you to do your best, or to work harder, you'll have a much better understanding of what that actually means—a barometer, if you will, by which to measure your own efforts against.

Let me sum it up in one very long sentence: *Those precious, exceptional, excellent few* know how to *focus*, do things with *purpose*, understand that their level of *investment* determines their level of return, are determined to put forth 100% of their *energy*, bring their *passion* to all things they do, accept full *responsibility* for their situation, endeavor to look and be *intelligent*, understand the importance of *gratitude*, *resolve* to do their absolute best till victory is achieved, and have a deep and profound *respect* for all things connected to the teaching/learning process. It's a winning formula, don't you think?

Before we can move on to our discussion concerning teachers, there is one last key, an extremely essential key—the Master Key, if you will, that we need to discuss. It is the *pièce de résistance* of operating in the realm of excellence. It's so important, I devoted an entire chapter to it, but first I'm sure you need to stretch your legs a bit. So, take a moment, bend over, and I'll see you on the next page.

Jazz Dancers, Inc. mid-1980s - Performance Photo: unknown
Dennon & Sayhber

CHAPTER SEVEN

THE MASTER KEY
THE LEADERSHIP OF SELF

"A good follower is a good leader!" In 1982, on one of the four Academy Awards shows I did, I had the privilege of working with the amazing Gregory Hines. What a talented performer he was. He was one of those iconic, quadruple-threat performers (dancer, singer, actor, choreographer) that anyone wishing to pursue Musical Theater just had to see. He earned Tony Award nominations for such Broadway shows as *Eubie*, and *Sophisticated Ladies*, and won the Tony Award for his work in *Jelly's Last Jam*. Sadly, he passed away in 2003 at the age of 57 due to liver cancer.

Fortunately for the world, he did several films showcasing both his acting and dancing skills. In one of the films he appeared in, *White Knights*, he co-starred with one of the Ballet world's iconic figures, Mikhail Baryshnikov. The pairing of these two was made even more spectacular because the choreography was supplied by another iconic figure from the Modern Dance world, Twyla Tharp. What a combination—Ballet meets Jazz/Tap meets Modern. In a film appropriately entitled *Tap*, you can see Hines with several of the genre's early pioneers—a must see for tap aficionados. He also appeared with his childhood performing partner, older brother Maurice, in the film *Cotton Club*. It's well worth your time viewing all these films.

Walter Painter, whom I learned a great deal from over the years, was choreographing a large-scale production number (a tribute to songwriter Harry Warren) that featured Hines and another talented dancer/singer Debbie Allen. There were to be several different dance styles used and one of them was, of course, Tap. Hines was a fascinating man and I became entranced as I watched him at every rehearsal. He was always on time, enthusiastic, and completely prepared to do whatever work was necessary in order to fully develop his performance. Talk about a work ethic! His love for his art was evident by his approach to the rehearsal process. He was a real "pro". I learned a great deal just by watching him.

I remember we were using canes in this one section and I was given the task of tossing Hines his cane as we men-type dancers made our entrance. Every rehearsal, I tossed that cane perfectly and he caught it just as he should. I felt pretty good about having been given this opportunity, for it meant the choreographer had confidence in me. Because this was going to be a live one-shot performance in front of the world, I did feel a certain amount of pressure. If I didn't toss it just right to him, he might drop it and look foolish. He'd look foolish and I be placed on the "do not call" list.

The night of the telecast, we approached that particular section and, just as I always did, I looked right at him, caught his eyes and tossed the cane. It went perfect -- couldn't have gone better -- at least that part. Immediatley after I tossed him his cane, mine slipped right out of my hand. Talk about embarrassment. I quickly retrieved my cane -- only a few million people across the globe may have noticed -- and continued on. Thankfully, the rest of the number continued without a hitch.

We had rehearsed that number, as well as the others we performed that evening, countless times during the previous couple weeks. Because the show was live, with no possibility of doing any "re-takes", we had to be super well prepared. My cane mishap notwithstanding, we dancers knew what we were required to do and, as professionals, we knew our jobs depended on it. In the professional world, being unfocused and irresponsible are unforgiveable sins.

By the way, I recently came across this number on YouTube. It's still a terrific number and, yes, I'm still embarrassed because no matter how many times I watch it, I still drop the darn cane.

Being responsible manifests itself in a purposeful intensity to conscientiously do whatever is required of one, and then some, to the best of one's ability. For dancers, that means no "marking". There could be no coasting through the rehearsal process—that's not what professionals do. For athletes, singers, dancers, actors, musicians and any other performing artist, the rehearsal period is where the polished performance is created.

"There's an old saying, I just made up, a long time ago, just the other day!" (Dennonism #18) Professionals are made long before they ever get paid. In other words, someone who is determined to become a professional thinks, acts and works like one long before anyone ever gives them the opportunity to be one. This applies to doctors, lawyers and business people as well. A person's attitude (remember Key # 7 regarding intelligence and perception of intelligence) about the very way they approach everything concerning their eventual profession determines whether or not they actually achieve their goal.

Mastering the key to leadership . . .

The same thing can be said about leadership. Leaders are made long before they're ever entrusted with a position of leadership. How? By demonstrating leadership skills on the one person they do -- or should -- have control over, themself. Those who demonstrate leadership skills on themselves cannot help but be recognized for it. It is something that stands out by virtue of its rareness. Stay with me as I explain what I mean.

In the previous chapter we examined *those precious, exceptional, excellent few* that have graced our classes over the years to find out what it is they do or possess that makes them operate at such a high level. We discovered "Ten Keys" that are common to each of them. As essential as these keys are in order to operate at an excellent level, they're not quite enough. There is one other, very important piece to the puzzle that must be acknowledged and embraced. I don't call it the eleventh key, but rather the "Master Key" because it is the key to unlocking the door of understanding and implementing all things "excellent".

The Master Key has to do with a specific kind of leadership. That's what we'll be examining in this chapter. Now before you turn me off because you have no real desire to be mayor, governor or king, hear me out.

• • DEFINITION TIME • •

Simply put . . . leaders cause things to happen. That's a very important word—"cause". It means "to make". Not in the sense of physical force, mind you, unless there is absolutely no alternative (I'll address that in a moment), but primarily through the use of highly-developed skills that encourage, motivate, and give incentive. Good leaders are "take charge" kind of people who aren't afraid of hard work and the responsibility that accompanies it.

Good leaders understand that they must first and foremost lead by example. They generally have highly-developed communication skills with the ability to inspire. They would not ask others to do and behave in such a way that they themselves do not, or at least have not, when they were in a similar position. They're usually knowledgeable (at least in terms of the situation they're in charge of) and highly efficient.

Whereas most individuals tend to see things only from a personal, subjective perspective, leaders have the ability to see the bigger picture. Their perspective is by nature broader in scope. They're capable of seeing beyond the moment to determine what needs to be done to achieve optimum results. This ability is absolutely essential for anyone desiring a position of authority.

They have an infectious passion for what they do that can't help but rub off on others. They do not allow those in their charge to operate in the dark. They keep them well informed on policies, procedures, and any changes that may be in the works. A good leader will make anyone and everyone who works for them believe they are as important to the proceedings at hand as they are—sometimes, even more important. When workers feel they are essential to the success of a given endeavor, their work effort improves dramatically.

Most importantly, a good leader fosters trust. He or she would never take undue advantage of others by misrepresenting his or her intentions. He or she understands his or her word represents who they are. In other words, they are their word. What they say is who they are. Trust is an essential component of any working relationship.

Self-leadership . . .

Though it may be true that not everyone is cut out to be a leader of many, everyone should be a leader of at least one—themself. Being a leader of one's self means taking charge of one's situation even when one is not the actual person in charge. It's all about taking a proactive role no matter what one's place is in an organization, a production, a class, a team, a family, etc., etc.

Being a leader does not necessarily mean being *the* leader. Though Gregory Hines was the star of the number we were doing on the Academy Awards Show, he was not the choreographer or director. In other words, he was not in charge. He did not select the music he was to dance to, choreograph the material, nor direct the camera shots for the piece. I'm not saying he did not have input. It's just that he had to follow the directions of several others all throughout the process of preparing his performance. Following directions is what everyone has to do, no matter what their position in an organization is. It's important to understand that following directions doesn't preclude exercising leadership.

"A good follower is a good leader!" (Dennonism #19) If leadership means causing things to happen, then self-leadership means causing things to happen to and for oneself. It's unfortunate, but the word "follower" has an undeserved, negative connotation. That's because there is no real understanding of what it means to be a follower—at least a good one. Contrary to popular belief, followers are not apathetic, lazy ne'er-do-wells that wait for things to happen to or for them. People who fall into that category aren't followers at all . . . they're people who've checked out and relinquished all responsibility for their lives to some undefined outside force. They don't follow well because doing so requires self-leadership.

I mentioned that, on a rare occasion, leadership might require some kind of physical coercion. This becomes necessary only when dealing with someone who will not cooperate—like when law enforcement apprehends a criminal, or a child acts out and words will simply not suffice, or when an unruly student disrupts the classroom by performing an obscene imitation of Lady Gaga and needs to be restrained.

Now, here's what I want everyone to understand. When any kind of physical force becomes necessary, it's only because the person in charge is dealing with someone who exercises no "self-leadership". Self-control is a form of leadership.

Outside force becomes necessary only when someone cannot or will not lead themself to do what's in the best interest of the situation, which then interrupts, disrupts, or screws up the proceedings, which in turn then leaves the person in charge with no other option than to take charge of the person who doesn't do it for themself. Fortunately this happens seldom, but when it does it is because the person who sits, stands, or dances in the "follower" position doesn't exercise leadership over his or her own actions.

To drill home the point, here's how I address such a student: **"If you can't lead yourself to be an attentive, responsive participant, then at least lead yourself out of the room!" (Dennonism #20)**

Important disclaimer . . .

Lest anyone think otherwise, let me stress here that good followers don't blindly follow anyone. Good followers are proactive industrious people who understand that their full physical, mental and emotional participation is necessary in order to learn, achieve, and grow.

Good following has nothing to do with accepting anything and everything someone says just because they are in charge. Au contraire . . . good followers know what they're doing and why, and take initiative to lead themselves to follow advice, directives and instruction that are given from qualified, knowledgeable, experienced "experts" in the field they are studying, or from their workplace manager. If the person in charge seems neither qualified nor knowledgeable, or if what they want from their followers is illegal, immoral or dangerous, they kick their self-leadership skills into high gear and hightail it out of there, pronto.

Shall we dance? . . .

What better way to illustrate the leadership skills necessary for someone to have in the follower's position than couple's dancing? In ballroom dancing there is the designated leader, which is traditionally the man's part, and the follower, which is traditionally the woman's part. Those of us who teach ballroom or Latin dancing realize that teaching someone to lead or follow is no easy task. Teaching the steps is one thing, but getting someone to understand what they need to do to be a good leader or follower takes a lot of time.

As I say to my female students, I cannot begin to lead them if they don't exercise strong self-leadership in their following. They have a role to play in the dance, and it's equally important as the man's. Their part requires them to make split-second decisions by being proactively attentive and responsive to their partner's lead. They cannot, even for a moment, let their mind wander. Though each partner has a job description (leader and follower), they both must take leadership over their part.

It's no different for the workplace, the classroom, or anywhere one finds oneself in the position of "follower". A good follower is a good leader of self who is fully engaged, smart, proficient and super-sensitive to the indicators the "leader" puts out.

The point is that self-leadership requires a thorough understanding of one's part in a given situation, and then taking the initiative to do it. It's the "doing" part that's important. Leaders are doers. Those who operate in the realm of excellence don't wait for some outside force to motivate them, or for the occasional, elusive "urge" to overwhelm them; they do it regardless of circumstances or feelings. Yes, it's great when one feels like it, and it's great when someone or something comes into play to inspire, but *those precious, exceptional, excellent few* don't wait. That's so important—they do not wait!

Self-leadership is the "Master Key" that's needed to take control over one's actions in order to operate in the fullness of excellence. For anyone wishing to be promoted or rewarded, you need to understand that those who are in a position to help you are already judging—sorry, evaluating what kind of leader -- self-leader -- you are. Believe me, excellence stands out. It stands out because it is so very rare. It's important to understand that before anyone will put you in a position of leading others, they'll take a good look to see how well you lead yourself.

Leadership on "speed" . . .

I've never been involved in any job where the ability to understand, take, and respond quickly to direction wasn't an essential, necessary component. If I ever wanted to work again for a particular choreographer, or director, I had to know what was expected of me and then exercise my self-leadership skills to show that I was focused, hard-working and reliable and . . . equally important, I was quick. In the world of "professional show business" speed is golden. As the cliche goes: "Time is money".

All teachers would love for their students to be quick, but few, I've found, actually teach the importance of the concept and then train their students in it. Yes, I'm advocating that instructors teach the lesson of **"taking direction quickly"** daily. Teachers need to constantly remind their students of its importance and call them on it whenever they're not doing so. No matter the subject matter, students need to learn how to listen, understand, receive, and respond quickly. There's a way to do this that requires exercising one's perception muscles to the max. Here's the thing . . .

THiNG # 24

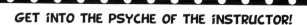

GET iNTO THE PSYCHE OF THE iNSTRUCTOR!

Learning how an instructor (anyone who's in charge) thinks, behaves and works is essential to becoming a quick responder. It requires learning to "read" another person to understand their desires, intentions and destinations, before they speak.

Being able to "read" another person demonstrates a high degree of awareness and intelligence relative to a workplace's particular method of operation. Remember, the classroom is a workplace too!

To get into the psyche of someone means to understand how someone thinks, what motivates them, what animates them—basically, it means to learn what makes that person "tick". That means learning their particular methods and procedures of operation, along with as many of their idiosyncrasies, foibles and peculiarities as you can.

The key to reading someone is learning to use your perception muscles to the max. Sayhber and I were trained early on in this concept. Our mentor, Steven Peck, did not like a lot of questions when he was conducting class or rehearsal. This made us have to work harder to know what he wanted and understand his intentions. Our having to work harder took on the form of having to intensify our focus (intense perceptive energy) on him and what he was doing. Since we couldn't do it verbally, we were forced to ask questions with our eyes and, in turn, receive answers the same way.

This served me well (my first audition experience notwithstanding) when I would work for other choreographers. If I could understand what a choreographer wanted by being purposefully perceptive during the beginning stages of the rehearsal process, I'd never find myself falling behind. I felt it was my responsibility to try to figure out what the choreographer wanted before he actually put it out there.

Yes, Matilda, there are dumb questions . . .

There is a well-known expression that says: "There are no dumb questions". Well, since I am bombarded with dumb questions every day, I highly beg to differ. What's a dumb question? It's one that demonstrates that you weren't exercising any self-leadership skills in focusing your attention, energy, and/or using your perception "muscles", so you missed the fact that the question you've just asked had just been answered! In other words, a dumb question is one that reveals to the instructor as well as all the other more attentive students that you are simply not paying attention.

Years ago I came up with my own expression that says if you're not fully engaged and fully exercising your perception "muscles" you are: **"Dumb as wood!" (Dennonism #21)** That basically means, if you're not focused enough to see and understand what's clearly being asked of you, you're no brighter than the floor you're standing on.

I do make allowances for beginners, where they may be legitimately suffering from "information overload" but, for the most part, students who ask "dumb" questions aren't looking for clarification anyway. They're either not paying attention (unfocused), or they are needy attention-seekers whose only way of getting noticed is by inappropriately interjecting themselves.

Students need to be taught (yes taught, because for most, it is not a natural thing to do) that by putting their full attention (brain power) solely 100% on the teacher, manager or parent, and using their eyes and ears to ask as well as answer any and all questions as they present themselves, they are then entering into the perceptive world of getting into the psyche of the teacher.

The question then arises, what kinds of questions should my eyes ask? How about this for starters: What is this particular teacher's method of communication, and how does it differ from other teachers I've had? How does he or she conduct the class (workplace environment), and how is it different from other teachers I've had? Did you notice that very important second part of each question, "how does it differ"? Every teacher has a particular approach, manner and method that sets him or her apart from others. Whether one way is better or worse is irrelevant. The point is that different teachers teach differently, and those differences need to be noticed, understood and adjusted to.

Another important question one can ask, and answer, with their eyes is: What is this particular teacher's energy level and how can I match it? That's an important skill. Be observant—it's never a good idea to operate too far above or below your teacher's intensity level.

A person's telling ways . . .

I'll let you in on a very important non-secret about teachers that most people never realize, but would greatly benefit from if they did. Here it is: all teachers (or managers, or bosses—basically all people, regardless of position) have a "way" about them that anyone can learn because, after a time (usually not very long), it reveals itself and becomes quite clear and therefore predictable. In the gambling world it's called a "tell". Poker players are looking for their opponent's "tells" to determine if they are bluffing. Yes, people are quite predictable in their "ways" and those ways can, and should, be learned. I'm astonished at how many students who never, no matter how many years they study with me, understand my method of operation.

As I said, I became quite aware of this as a working dancer when, over the course of weeks, months and years, I would work for many different choreographers, all of whom had very distinct, different personalities, as well as different methods of working, not to mention different dance styles. It was not any one of the choreographer's responsibilities to figure me out. It was up to me to figure them out. How I acted in the rehearsal setting depended on whom I was working for. I would always exercise my self-leadership skills by being professional, conscientious and diligent, but my professionalism manifested itself differently for each personality I worked for—that's being "smart".

Waiting is the antithesis of self-leadership . . .

Though most students and workers who enter a workplace environment for the very first time generally wait for someone to tell them what to do, self-leaders do not. What's a person supposed to do if they've not yet been instructed to do anything?

If you're a proactive, self-leader, you'll begin looking for any and all signs that might reveal the teacher's, or manager's particular "way". It's called casing the joint, which is old-time gangster talk meaning visually perusing the room, taking in and digesting any and all information that may be relevant to how the instructor operates, or wants you to operate. A lot is revealed in what is displayed. There may be pictures, drawings, or quotations from scholars that give some indication of what the class and the instructor is all about.

Hanging out and doing nothing until you are practically forced to do something makes what our Steven Peck called a real: **"Baccala!". (Steven's saying #6)** From what I gather, a baccala is Sicilian for dead codfish, which basically means you're a pathetic, lazy blob. Believe me, being called a baccala by Steve was not a pleasant thing.

People who learn to "read" people get along and prosper much better in the classroom, their jobs, their social, and family life. Students who learn to "read" their teachers and subsequently adjust their ways of working will most certainly prosper better than those who don't.

Mirror, mirror on the wall . . .

Dancers should be asking, and answering for themselves, which arm, leg, and body position is the instructor doing? I know, duh, seems kind of obvious. Well, many a time, I've stood in front of a class doing a particular position and a student or two or three standing directly behind me is so enthralled in watching themselves in the mirror, they miss what I'm doing entirely. The worst part is they are completely oblivious to it.

It's then that I inform my students that learning to dance, especially in the beginning stages, is pretty much 100% imitation. That means they should be looking mostly at me, or my assistants, and seldom at themselves. To drill home the point I'll instruct everyone to stare directly at themself in the mirror, at which time I state: **"When you look at yourself in the mirror, you're looking at the person who least knows what to do!" (Dennonism # 22)** Conversely, I'll tell them that when they look at me, or one of my assistants, they're looking at the person, or persons who most knows what to do. So, get out of the mirror and start imitating me!"

Dancers should be asking themselves what's the "feel" or phrasing the teacher wants for a particular exercise, movement pattern, or combination. Listen closely to the music being used and how it relates to the movement/steps given. I've noticed that many, even the more advanced students, often don't grasp the particular "feel" a teacher wants. What all too often happens is they dance the way they've always danced, you know, by habit, which usually means the way their previous primary or favorite teacher did. (We're back to Thing # 18: "All habits are bad habits".)

Are questions ever acceptable? . . .

Now, before you get all excited, I'm not saying there is never a time to ask questions. On the contrary, there are times, but students ask many unnecessary questions that only serve to reveal their lack of focus. Questions of clarification are generally fine but, even if one has an appropriate question, one should be aware that there is a right time and a wrong time to speak up. Wrong time? Yes, remember to look for the time when a teacher is open to questions.

Many a time, I'm in the middle of a creative moment, when my attention is on developing an idea pertaining to choreography, or I might be in the middle of developing a point of instruction (for which the level of profundity is no-doubt immeasurable) and someone breaks that concentration, thereby stifling my creative/profound moment (moments that cannot be easily retrieved) by asking a question that I would have eventually gotten around to pre-answering had the student let me get that far.

So students, first and foremost, listen and watch to see if your question has already been answered or might be answered in due order. When you begin asking and answering questions without ever opening your mouth, you'll begin transforming your-self into one of those "smart" people that every teacher dreams about. If your concerns aren't addressed and looks like they won't be, then look and wait for the teacher to signal in some way that he or she is open for questions.

Conclusion . . .

The "master key" to operating in the realm of excellence is excercising leader-ship over oneself. Excellence does not just happen. Those who operate at a level beyond the "norm" do so because they are proactive self-leaders. They are those "take-charge" kind of people who understand that leadership -- the leadership of self -- is the "master key" that opens the door to all things excellent. It's not good enough just to know what one ought to do. One must exercise leadership over oneself in order to actually *do* what one knows to do.

I summed up the previous chapter with a very long sentence by explaining what those who operate in the realm of excellence know, understand, and do. By changing the verbs "know", "understand", and "do" to "lead" it becomes clearer as to how these pre-cious few actually accomplish what they do. Read it this time with the changes and see what I mean.

Those precious, exceptional, excellent few, lead themselves to **focus**, *lead* them-selves to do things with **purpose**, *lead* themselves to fully **invest**, *lead* themselves to put forth 100% of their **energy**, *lead* themselves to stoke their **passion**, *lead* themselves to accept full **responsibility** for their situation, *lead* themselves to look and be **intelligent**, *lead* themselves to be **grateful**, *lead* themselves to **resolve** to do their absolute best till victory is achieved, and *lead* themselves to **respect** all things connected to the teaching/learning process. Then, to top it all off, the *pièce de résistance,* they *lead* themselves to **get into the psyche** of their instructors.

We could shorten that very long sentence to this: *Those precious, exceptional, excellent few,* **lead** themselves!

In Act Three -- as I've continually alluded to -- I'm going to be speaking di-rectly to and about my fellow instructors. Though it's directed mainly toward instructors, it's completely relevant to anyone who operates in a position of leadership and authority. I'm talking managers and bosses of all kinds. Take a moment and relieve your tension by doing a few head rolls and shoulder rolls . . . then grab yourself a tootsie roll and I'll meet you over in the next act.

ACT THREE

Clearing The Air!
- The Sweet Smell Of Respect -

Some Came Running 1958 - MGM Still Photo
Steven Peck center, with Carmen Phillips, Frank Sinatra, Shirley MacLaine, Dean Martin

Steven Peck and Lita Leon - Hollywood Latin Dance Team
Performing at Steve's Night Club, Club Seville - Circa late 1950's

CHAPTER EIGHT
TEACHER VERSUS EDUCATOR
TAKING CARE OF THE QUARTER NOTES!

"**Who do you have to thank for how good you look when you get naked at night?**" Mr. Steven Peck, otherwise known as Stefano Ignazio Apostle Pecoraro, was a provocative guy to say the least. I've already mentioned his Sicilian heritage and how that influenced his whole attitude on life and the arts. He attracted a lot of people to him because of his dynamic passion for everything he set his mind to. He also tended to annoy some with his straightforward, no nonsense way of communicating. This man was always doing something -- building something, creating something, changing something -- always working to improve things. Status quo was not in his vocabulary. Whatever he did, he put his entire heart, soul, and mind into it. As I said at his memorial, right before Sayhber and I did a short Mambo to tribute our beloved "creative father": "He's the only person that ever made me feel lazy!"

Many of us young aspiring dancers had numerous opportunities to listen to him pontificate on the issues of art, dance, acting, and food (food was an important aspect of his life). It was always fun to hear stories of his MGM days, where he was under contract as an actor. He had the good fortune to work for some of the great directors of Hollywood's Golden Era. One of his early films, *Some Came Running*, was directed by Liza's father, Vincente Minnelli—noted for such films as *An American In Paris*, and *Gigi*. In *Some Came Running*, Steven played Shirley MacLaine's gangster boyfriend whose crazed jealously over her interest in Frank Sinatra led him to unintentionally (he was aiming at Sinatra) kill her at the end of the movie. It was an important film that catapulted him into the big leagues of Hollywood.

I mention Liza Minnelli, because almost twenty years after Steven Peck made his first film at MGM, I made my first film at MGM. My film was *New York, New York* and it starred Liza, along with Robert DeNiro, and was directed by Martin Scorsese. Once again I was hired by my good buddy, Broadway -- now Hollywood -- choreographer Ron Field. Having heard stories about MGM from Steve, it was fun to find myself on the very same lot, in the very same sound stages, on the very same floor where the likes of Gene Kelly and Fred Astaire, as well as Liza's mother, Judy Garland, once worked.

One day, Steve and I were walking around the outside of his Orange County, CA dance studio, when he stopped to pick up a tiny piece of paper. It was something I would have walked right by. As he did so, he said: "These are the quarter notes." Quarter notes? "Yea," he explained, "you got to take care of the little things, which all add up to the big things." This happened around the time the studio was being set up, and all of us who were involved in his dance company were enlisted to help build, paint and generally ready the place for business. In preparing the business, he was acutely aware of the necessity to care for all aspects, regardless of size.

It was during this time, I came to realize that no job was ever too small or menial for him to personally take part in. If he asked us to do something, like move boxes, or sweep out, or paint or whatever, he was right there leading the way. He never asked anyone to do something he himself wasn't prepared to do. That alone proved to be one of the greatest lessons in leadership I've ever had.

As I look back, I find it completely fascinating that many of the things I learned from him had nothing to do with dance, and yet everything to do with dance. What they really had to do with was life. Most everything I learned from him helped me become a better me, and yes, I'll say it, an even "smarter" me. Steven Peck was not an educated man in the formal sense of the word. What he was, though, was a self-motivated, highly intense, very determined, self-educated man.

He had been a New York kid who worked his way out of the streets to make a successful career as a dancer, choreographer, nightclub owner, dance studio owner, and Hollywood actor, appearing in dozens of films and TV shows, not to mention his countless stage appearances. In his later years, he became a successful businessman and restaurateur creating the very popular Angelo's & Vinci's Italian Restaurant in Fullerton, CA. The restaurant is still there and, by the way, if you'd like to see an amazing photo collection of Steve's career, as well as a bunch of early photos of Sayhber and me dancing with the Steven Peck Jazz Dance Company, stop on by there, have a pizza, and check out the historic wall of photos.

In addition to everything else, he and partner/wife Cynthia were involved in various philanthropic ventures. He was the kind of man who took pleasure in helping his family as well as others. He was also very appreciative for his successes. There was never a time we visited him that he would not express his gratitude to God and us, for all his blessings, the most important being the love of his life, Cynthia. After he passed away in 2005, Cynthia has continued their tradition of blessing others.

Though Steven Peck possessed no letters after his name, you know, like B.A., M.A., or Ph.D., he did possess a thirst for knowledge and a strong desire to better himself, and an equally strong desire to pass on the knowledge and wisdom he acquired (be it about dance, the arts, business, or just life in general) to anyone who chose to be associated with him.

I used to say Steven Peck was always teaching you, but I've since amended that. I now say, he was always educating you.

A distinction with a big difference . . .

That brings me to what this chapter is all about. At the risk of offending many in the teaching profession, I'm going to make a distinction that most do not make. I've been using the word teacher or instructor up to now, but what I have really been talking about is something more.

Admittedly, in the world of academia, everyone who teaches is considered an "educator". It is presumed that if you have received your college degree and teaching credentials, and have been hired by an official learning institution, then you may be considered an educator. Though it may be technically so, I've been around long enough to see that, in reality, it ain't necessarily so.

So what's the big deal? Why do I feel the need to clarify the differences? First, I want those who truly are "educators" to be identified, understood, and credited for their special contribution. Second, I hope to inspire those just entering the teaching profession to work at achieving real educator status.

There's the teacher . . .

Simply put, a teacher is one who regurgitates information to others they themselves have learned in order to accomplish a given task, perform a duty, or retain material long enough to pass a test. They are strictly subject-matter oriented. That's important, let me say it again—a teacher is strictly subject-matter oriented. Their only concern is having their students do the requisite work that has been mandated by the school district or institution they work for. In the area of dance, a teacher would only be concerned with teaching the basic techniques of a given discipline.

What's important to understand is that a teacher has a narrowly focused viewpoint of his or her job. That's also very important; so let me say that again—a teacher has a narrowly focused viewpoint of what his or her job is. As they see it, their job is solely to teach their subject, and if the students get it, great, and if they don't, well, c'est la vie.

I realize that there is hardly a teacher anywhere who believes that their focus is narrow. That's because they haven't really put much thought into it, and that, most likely, is because they themselves have no idea there is a distinction to be made. After all, they're already referred to as "educator" by their schools, unions and fellow compadres. So, what's wrong with that? If a teacher is teaching his or her subject well (more or less), what more can you ask for? I'm all for teachers who teach well. It's just that there are those who operate on a different level -- on a higher plane, if you will -- whose contribution soars high above your average, everyday teacher.

Then there's the educator . . .

The educator has a big-picture viewpoint of what his or her job is. What that means is the educator is as much concerned with the individual's growth as a human being as he or she is with their learning any prescribed material. The growth to which I'm referring extends way beyond basic "brain" knowledge. What I'm talking about is character development. I'm talking about leaving behind one's childish ways and embracing the more difficult, more mature, adult ways. That all has to do with the monumentally important concept of responsibility, which is what I spoke about in the previous couple chapters—the idea of "excellence".

The educator will constantly force (I use that word on purpose) his or her students to examine themselves to see whether they are doing all that they could, or should, do. It may sound a little metaphysical but, by his or her very demeanor, as well as his or her methods, the educator holds up a kind of mirror to students, forcing them to take a good look at who and what they are.

I've studied dance, choreography, acting, and singing from many different teachers, all of whom had something to offer, but very few of them would I credit with the designation of "educator". They taught me important techniques, steps and choreography -- all good stuff -- but for the most part, that was it. The same could be said for my academic classes in school. Most of my teachers' teachings were strictly subject-matter oriented. There were a few, however, who took it upon themselves to help me, and anyone else who'd allow it, to grow up.

Life lessons . . .

I believe that using the word "educator" when referring to anyone who teaches only diminishes the value of the word, just as bestowing the title of "artist" on anyone who ever drew a picture diminishes that word. The title "educator" should be reserved for those who actually deserve it by virtue of having earned it, which, more often that not, takes maturation. Just as fine vintage wines increase in quality and value over many years, so too can a teacher who spends years on the "battlefield" (classroom) working to refine their methods and techniques.

Ask any teacher who's been around a good long while whether they're any better at their job than they were when they began. Ask the battle-scarred teacher if they know more now about what it takes to communicate than they did when they first began. The day-to-day, hand-to-hand "combat" (teaching) a teacher endures over time bestows a certain knowledge and wisdom that cannot be otherwise obtained. I use military, warfare terminology on purpose. The soldier who's seen combat a number of times has a lot more practical knowledge than the recently graduated recruit.

Part of the wisdom that's gained from years on the "battlefield" is a realization that the needs of the student far exceed the basic requirements of giving lectures, handing out assignments, and grading papers. That's important—the "needs of the student". Educators seize upon opportunities as they arise to teach their charges on matters that transcend the particular subject they're studying. These are generally referred to as "life lessons". "Life lessons" are lessons that not only help the student to become a much better student, but also, more importantly, help him or her become a much better person. It's all about preparing a student for real life (life after school, when every decision and action takes on monumental importance) by helping them understand that it is their life, and they are responsible for it. This is the "bigger-picture viewpoint" I spoke of earlier.

I'll be giving some wonderful examples of true educators in a bit, so stay with me.

Some wines just spoil . . .

Let's be clear about one thing—having taught for many years does not automatically qualify one as an educator. In other words, time is not the be-all, end-all determinant. Wines that are not cared for properly do not age well—they simply spoil. There are many who teach for years who never achieve "educator" status. They're the kind of teacher that only does what is minimally required. They give assignments, lecture on material, grade papers, and demonstrate to their dance students the correct way to execute a given exercise. They are perfectly content to clock in and out, just like a factory worker doing the same mundane job day after day.

By the sheer routine of their schedule, this kind of teacher is often uninspired and passionless. They've allowed themselves to become routine in everything they do. That's the problem, they're routine -- which is another way of saying they're bored -- and we all know a bored teacher is a boring teacher. It's a case where an experienced teacher has let their many years on the "battlefield" wear them down to the point of giving up. Not giving up on the basic rudiments of teaching necessarily, just giving up on doing anything above and beyond.

The person who is absolutely determined to make a positive difference in an individual's life by going above and beyond the basic requirements of the job, is the person who deserves to be called educator. Like an artist, they see what they do as more of a calling than a job. It's not in the educator's DNA to be routine—they don't just clock in.

Unlike your average, everyday teacher, the primary concern of an educator is to facilitate the development of his or her students' character. They know that the more developed their students' character becomes, the easier their job will be to teach them whatever subject it is they teach.

When challenging my students on matters of character, I tell them point blank: **"I want to send you to your next teacher a better student than when you came to me!"** (Dennonism #23) I'm absolutely determined to make my students' next teacher's job easier. That would be the greatest compliment to me—not that a student of mine is recognized for his or her wonderful dancing ability, though that'd be nice, but rather is recognized for being an exceptionally conscientious, hard-working, maybe even "smart", student.

Now, I want to be real here, educators want and need to be paid, but it is not their financial recompense that motivates them to work beyond their basic job description. It's the gratification and fulfillment that comes from having made a real difference in a person's life.

Bond beyond friendship . . .

Some teachers have the ability to connect with their students in a deep and profound way. They strive to make that connection knowing that, without it, their ability to teach is hindered. It's a bond that has little to do with friendship and more to do with two infinitely more important things—trust and respect. If an instructor gains trust and respect from his or her students, they are more likely to be engaged and responsive.

I'm about to say something that is sure to offend some in the teaching profession so, if you're the squimish sort, you may want to cover your eyes before you read this. There has been a troubling trend over the past 20 or 30 years. I see teachers increasingly doing anything and everything they can in order to become their student's friend. You see this manifest itself in the way some teachers dress, talk, and act. If it weren't for the receding hairlines, wrinkles, and sagging backsides, one would be hard-pressed to tell the difference between student and teacher.

Instead of presenting an example of maturity and dignity for a student to emulate and aspire to, they lower themselves by adopting the student's fashion, dialect, and attitude—all for the misguided purpose of acceptance. As I see it, the desire to be a student's friend stems from a couple of erroneous notions. First, the teacher believes that if they look, talk, and act like their students, they'll be thought of as the "cool" teacher, which, in their mind, means acceptance, which, still further in their mind, means motivated, hard-working students. Second, the teacher still possesses an immature, adolescent need to be liked by everyone, so dressing like their students is their way of showing solidarity. Sorry to have to say this, but for a teacher, this is a childish way to think and behave. It's children who need to belong, and it's children who get extremely uncomfortable when someone doesn't like them, not adults.

It's this kind of thinking that results in a reluctance to impose rules, boundaries, and discipline (hey, it works for Cesar Millan), not to mention setting high standards for which the student must live up to. After all, your friends don't keep you from doing things you like, no matter how stupid, do they? Well actually, a true friend will but, all too often, your equally stupid peers won't . . . and that's exactly what a teacher is not, or should not be—a peer!

The "mature" understand there will always be those who don't like them and it's not necessarily a reflection on them. You see the same disturbing trend of "trying to be a friend" in a lot of parents these days. Wanting or needing to be your student or child's friend - - when what they really need is a strong, wise, Yoda-like sage -- isn't really helping them.

The educator's job is to challenge, stimulate, prompt, urge, push and prod students to move past their own inherent complacency, whether or not they like it or the educator. To quote the former director of one college dance department I work for, who is now the current head of another college dance department -- a person known for his super positive, dynamic energy and motivating personality -- Mr. Daniel Berney: "If you don't tick off a few students, you're not doing something right".

I, as I'm sure most teachers do, endeavor to be the kindest, sweetest person in the world, but there are times when the need to be strong and direct is the only course of action that'll work. When confronted with an apathetic, unengaged student I have a choice to make—either do something or do nothing. Anyone in charge of anything, or anyone, knows they have to pick their battles; otherwise, they'd be in a perpetual state of combat. That said, I generally choose to do something. When my being nice and polite doesn't work, I'll increase the intensity of my voice and physical demeanor to whatever is necessary. I may even choose to use more direct, somewhat piercing, verbiage in order to capture and center the student's attention.

At that point, I'm not concerned with being my student's friend. More precisely, I'm not concerned with whether or not my student, in all his or her immature glory, will like me for what I'm doing. I'm concerned with him or her grasping an important concept, point, or idea that just might change that student's life. If you really think about it, at that moment am I not being my student's very best friend? Though it may seem perplexing to some in the beginning, my experience has taught me that the overwhelming majority of my students, over time, see that I do have their best interest at heart.

Another aspect of trust comes from a consistency in the teacher's approach and rhetoric that can be counted on. In other words, the instructor says what he or she means and means what he or she says, and then stays consistent! Students in classes, as well as workers in offices, want and need to understand what their teachers or bosses want and need from them. When a student or worker can rely on their teacher or boss to act in a consistent, dependable way, the seed of trust begins to grow. A major aspect of leadership is dependability. Can I count on my leader (teacher, boss, manager, parent) to be consistent, or do I have to dance on eggs constantly figuring out what he or she wants from me each and every day?

The Princess Syndrome . . .

There is a good percentage of students who are quite adept at the art and science of manipulation. These young ones (and not so young ones) know exactly what to say and how to say it in order to get some kind of special consideration—which basically means to get their way. I call it the "Princess Syndrome".

This kind of student (female or male) has an entitlement attitude, as if she (or he) were born of royalty, giving her (or him) many privileges that mere commoners could never expect. This generally means that a deadline for assignments, adhering to rules and protocols, or working to one's fullest capacity simply doesn't apply to them because they're "special". It's unfortunate, but too often teachers, under the guise of being "sensitive" and "compassionate", let themselves be manipulated (fooled) to accommodate this kind of student.

Please know, I'm not talking about rare instances of grave matters, which do call for special consideration. I'm talking about the student or worker who has a hundred and one excuses for constantly being tardy, not being fully engaged, doing poor work, or not doing the work at all.

The educator (be they parent, teacher, or boss) will not be deterred or dissuaded by their student's manipulative efforts to get out of doing something. Neither will he or she be angered or hurt by the occasional childish outburst of "I hate you!" The seasoned, mature adult knows it's only an emotional outburst based on an immature, childish view of what the student thinks they deserve—in other words, the "Princess Syndrome".

Learning how to learn how to learn . . .

The educator makes it known to his or her students that they are in a perpetual state of learning how to learn. Whether a given subject seems relevant or important to a student (often a student does not have the maturity to know what is, or will be, relevant to their futures anyway) is not the primary concern of the educator. Their primary concern is for the student to grasp the concept that when learning a given subject, it is an exercise in and of itself in "learning how to learn how to learn", and that's good!

That means teaching our students to embrace (not necessarily loving or having fun with) the work that's involved in order to learn a given subject, complete a project, or perform a duty.

Understand now, I'm addressing primarily the subjects that we don't (at least at first) take to very easily. It's rather like eating vegetables; it's important, but not always fun, or easy, or pain-free! It doesn't take any convincing to get someone to eat pizza, or burgers, or sweets, but the veggies—that's a different story. The educator understands human nature and the tendency to gravitate toward the academic sweets and shun the more difficult, more important, academic veggies.

It's the educator's job to get across to his or her students that shunning the difficult in favor of the fun, or easy, or pain-free is a sure pathway to stagnation, and ultimate failure in life. It's also the educator's job to get across to his or her students that any given challenge set before them, whether it's perceived to be necessary or relevant, represents every future challenge they may face. The student's ability to work through the difficult learning process in one area is a good indicator of how they will work in all other areas. (Remember Steven's Saying #4: "How you are in dance is how you are in life, and how your are in life is how you are in dance!")

The educator's challenge is to get across to the student that the question set before them is not: "Do I like this subject and is it going to be fun?", but rather: "Do I have the ability, capacity, and tenacity to learn this subject, regardless of its "fun", "easy", or "pain-free" appeal?" Again, it's all about "learning how to learn how to learn" and it's only by working through the difficult challenges of learning something that does not, at least at first, come easily that one's "learning muscles" grow strong.

Personally, I'll use anything within my means to inspire my classes to work beyond their perceived capabilities. If appealing to their sense of pride and self-respect doesn't work, I'll appeal to their personal vanity. When the class is engaged in a particularly grueling exercise that I know will produce amazing physical results if they'll only keep at it, I'll blurt out: **"Who do you have to thank for how good you look when you get naked at night?" (Dennonism #24)**

A willingness to engage in whatever work is necessary reveals something very important about a person's character. In the olden days, (days before my time), if you were a person who did not shun responsibility and embraced the work involved in whatever situation you found yourself, no matter how tedious or difficult, you were thought to be a person of high moral character. Sayhber's and my parents' generation, often referred to as the "greatest generation", exemplified that very concept. Out of necessity, our dads worked six, sometimes seven, days a week, and sometimes worked multiple jobs to support their families. There were no handouts in those days, not that they would have taken them. No job was too menial. For that generation, dignity came in the form of self-reliance.

That's such an important point, let me highlight it: Dignity comes from self-reliance. To my knowledge, my father, Jack Rawles, and Sayhber's father, Al Snyder, never ever thought about self-esteem. It was respect they were after and it was respect they earned—from their families, their peers, and yes, even from themselves.

Several years ago there was someone who, for a short time, headed a college dance department where I taught. When confronted with her lackadaisical approach to teaching, as well as her somewhat aloof attitude toward her students, she lamented her frustration by saying: "What am I supposed to be, a cheerleader?"

Teachers need to understand that it is to their advantage to be energized, animated, and extremely passionate when conducting class. Energy begets energy, so if that means grabbing a pair of pom-poms and jumping in the air, I'm all for it. Here's the thing . . .

THiNG # 25

From obscurity to relevancy . . .

Real educators (again, not necessarilty your average, everyday teacher) tend to be extremely passionate and enthusiastic about their subject matter, which enlivens and invigorates the classroom, which in turn motivates many of the most apathetic students. They also have the ability to make a subject relevant, no matter how obscure it may seem on the surface. I've had students telling me how agonizing it is to be in a class (dance or otherwise) where the teacher is low-key, passionless, and just plain dull.

It certainly requires much more energy and effort from a teacher to be constantly energized and animated, but it is the most effective way to get students engaged in the process. It's also extremely important for teachers to convey the relevancy of what they're teaching. All too often, teachers leave their subject matter in the theoretical realm. That finally brings us to . . .

Educator example time . . .

Let's look at two outstandingly brilliant examples of people whose methods of operation catapulted them from your average everyday teacher status to superstar educator status.

Example #1: JAIME ALFANSO ESCALANTE GUITERREZ

A perfect example of someone who relayed the relevancy of his subject matter in an excited, highly passionate manner was a man named Jaime Escalante. He gained a lot of notoriety for his success teaching Algebra and Calculus at Garfield High in East Los Angeles from 1974 to 1991. I ask you, what could be a more boring, irrelevant subject to a teenager in a lower economic, urban center than higher math?

Though it took some doing, he ultimately gained his students', as well as peers', respect with his passionate and innovative methods. Using very creative means, this man was able to convey to many of his students that they could take control of their futures and climb out of their current meager existence and find employment in engineering, electronics, and computers. That's extremely important. He was determined to get his charges to understand that what they were doing in his classroom had a direct connection to their futures.

He miraculously achieved what no others had before him by conveying the relevancy of learning higher math to a group of students who otherwise wouldn't have cared. While other teachers were busy teaching math because the district mandated it, he was busy teaching math for the sake of his students' futures.

To many, especially at first, his methods (dare I say "techniques") seemed completely unorthodox. Nonetheless, they proved to be extremely successful. Remember how I said educators don't just clock in and out. Well, he was chastised for coming in too early and leaving too late. He was even threatened with dismissal if he continued doing so. Imagine that—he was criticized for caring too much and working too hard. Nothing irritates a lazy, complacent teacher more than when someone, who by their hard work, dedication, and enthusiasm, makes them look bad.

In 1982, he came to national prominence when an astonishing high number of his high school students passed the Advanced Placement Calculus exam. Their success was so astonishing that they were accused of cheating. They were not, of course, and were soon cleared of all charges when they retook the test with similar results.

When sharing with other teachers, he said: "The key to my success with youngsters is a very simple and time-honored tradition: hard work for the teacher and student alike". Here's a case of leading by example. He was willing to work extremely hard, far beyond the dictates of his job description, to demonstrate to his students (and fellow teachers) how learning works—actually, how life really works. His success caught the attention of many around the country, including President Ronald Reagan.

His success working with inner-city kids was so amazing that in 1988 author Jay Mathews wrote a book entitled *Escalante: The Best Teacher in America*. That same year a movie was made about him. In the film, *Stand and Deliver*, actor Edward James Olmos did an outstanding job portraying Escalante, a man who didn't just want to teach, but was determined to better the lives of his students. If you want to see what an educator looks like, check out the film.

Example #2: JOHN ROBERT WOODEN

Another high-profile example of an educator comes in the guise of an exceptionally inspiring man beloved as much for his methods of instructing as he was for the results he achieved. He was world-renowned teacher, coach and educator, John Wooden. Wooden led the UCLA Bruins mens basketball team from 1948 to 1975. In 2003, he was awarded the Presidential Medal of Freedom and, in 2009, he was named The Sporting News "Greatest Coach of All Time". He has received countless awards for his outstanding contribution to the world of basketball.

Okay, he was a great basketball coach, how does that make him an educator? There are so many testimonies of his unique methods from his students who've subsequently gone on to their own fame and fortune. Bill Walton, David Meyers and Kareem Abdul Jabbar are but a few who credit John Wooden with so much of their ultimate success, not just for what they were able to accomplish as professional athletes, but also for what they were able to acheive in every area of life.

In his 2004 book *My Personal Best*, Wooden conveys the lessons he learned from a journey that spanned some 90-plus years. He also relates the teaching methods (techniques?) and tools he used to teach his players to be the winners they became. He developed what he called the "Pyramid of Success". It's a fantastic teaching tool that is designed to help anyone, athlete or not, understand what the very concept of success means.

Among his more famous maxims are: "Failing to prepare is preparing to fail" and "Be quick, but don't hurry". A couple of my favorite quotes from the book are: "Discipline yourself and others won't have to" and "It's what you learn after you know it all that counts". There are so many wonderful life lessons in his book. I highly recommend it to anyone who wishes to better themselves. I especially recommend it to aspiring educators.

John Wooden passed away on June 4th, 2010, just shy of his 100th birthday. Though recognized as having created the winningest college basketball team ever, for him, satisfaction came from having been a part of molding young men into responsible, caring, hard-working individuals who knew how to be winners in a more important game called life. Now that's an educator.

No B.A., M.A., or Ph.D. required . . .

I am an advocate of higher education, but it's important to know that many of the most successful entrepreneurs, politicians, filmmakers, painters, dancers and athletes never went to or completed college. Can you say Walt Disney, Wolfgang Puck, Abraham Lincoln, Dave Thomas, Mary Kay, Michael Dell, Steve Jobs, Bill Gates, Mikhail Baryshnikov, and the inimitable Foghorn Leghorn? The practical insights, wisdom, and skills these people (and many others) offer to anyone wishing to learn are incalculable. As a matter of fact, much of what these people have to offer—you can't get from a university.

My point is you don't have to sit in the office or position of "teacher" to be considered an educator. (That ought to aggravate many in the academic world.) What it takes is a "calling" to pass on one's wisdom and knowledge (however acquired), along with a real desire to better the lives of others. Simply put, it is my contention that it's not the official designation of teacher that makes one an educator.

Conclusion . . .

Let me finish up by getting back to the teacher's need to be their student's friend concept. Both Sayhber and I have found a certain irony in the fact that the less we're concerned with being our student's friend, the more our students wish to be our friends. It all goes back to my original assertion that it is much more important to gain a students' trust and respect. John Wooden and Jaime Escalante didn't set out to be their students' friends. Nor did our beloved Steven Peck. Their desire was to impact their students' lives in a great and profound way, and for that, they eventually became the very best of friends with many of their students. Remember, true friendship is based on trust and respect.

Sayhber and I evaluate our success as educators not only by how much our students' skills have improved, but also, more importantly, whether or not they've become more responsible, focused self-leaders. Do they now think differently, which translates into acting differently, than before? Has their overall work ethic improved? In other words, are they better understanding and embracing the "Ten Keys To Excellence"?

Once again, the primary difference between your average everyday teacher and the educator is that the educator's teachings transcend the subject matter. They see the learning of their subject as a metaphor for learning anything. They're concerned with teaching their students how to take charge of their own learning, and subsequently their own lives. When someone becomes a better, more responsible student, there is no stopping him or her.

Though you can't win them all, you can put forth your best effort and help as many as will let you. Our Steven Peck still took a certain amount of pride when lamenting about someone who never fully measured up. I can still hear him saying: **"I still got more out of him (or her) than anyone else!" (Steven's saying #7)** That's what qualified him as an educator. He didn't just teach dance, or acting—his goal was to get the very best effort possible from anyone who'd put his or her trust in him.

In the final two chapters I'm going to get into some specifics of what educators do in order to create an environment that brings about optimum conditions for teaching and learning. But, before you turn the page, you may want to freshen your drink.

Stephano Apostlé
presents the
vital dynamic
STEVEN PECK DANCE COMPANY

Sayhber "Sares" and Steven Peck 1971
Performing "T.C. Rock" a jazz/rock Tango
Photo: Unknown

CHAPTER NINE
CREATING AN ENVIRONMENT OF EXCELLENCE
EXCELLENCE 101!

"Nice doesn't mean good!" Back in 1992, our concert dance company, Jazz Dancers, Inc. (JDI), was invited to perform at the Jazz Dance World Congress held at Northwestern University in Evanston, IL, just outside of Chicago. This was and still is an event hosted by Giordano Jazz Dance Chicago. It's quite a prestigious affair with dancers coming from all over the world to participate. There were master classes given by some of the best-known figures in Jazz dance at the time, including Gus Giordano, Frank Hatchett, Joe Tremaine, and Matt Mattox. There were also performances given by several different companies, one having come from as far away as Japan.

JDI was set to perform a couple of works from our repertoire: one entitled "Take Another Five", a classical Jazz piece; and, "Mambo Fantasy", a Latin/Salsa/Jazz piece. We were excited to be there, demonstrating the kind of Jazz dance we were noted for. We were also happy to be there to see and meet some of the dance world's iconic figures. We had already known Joe Tremaine for many years and it was good to see him again. He's someone we have great respect for, and whose reputation and honored place in the area of Jazz dance is well deserved.

In between rehearsals for our performance, we went around to watch some of the classes being offered . . . you know, to see what gems these elder statesmen had to offer. All of the classes were good, but there was one class that will forever be etched in my memory. It was taught by the incredible Matt Mattox. Mattox had been there from the very beginning of the development of Theater/Jazz dance. Aside from his brilliant teaching, he was also respected in the industry for his work as a performer on Broadway, television, and in films.

We were anxious to meet him because he was yet another link -- Broadway/Hollywood guy Ron Field being the other -- to the man credited with being the "father" of Jazz dance, Jack Cole. As a matter of fact, he had been a protégé of Cole's and worked for him many times. He also worked for many of the other great choreographers of his time including one of my very favorites, Michael Kidd. You can see Mattox featured performing in many films, including *Seven Brides For Seven Brothers* (choreographed by Kidd) and *Gentleman Prefer Blondes* (choreographed by Cole).

I wanted to meet him not only for his connection with Jack Cole, but also because we had a couple things in common. We had both worked for Michael Kidd, and we both had partnered the beautiful Cyd Charisse. Though you can't see me partner Cyd (because it was in her nightclub act where video taping was prohibited), you can see Mattox partner Cyd in the film, *The Bandwagon*. Oh yeah, you can also catch that other great dancer, Fred Astaire partnering Cyd. I was anxious to ask him a question or two about his time with the infamous Jack Cole.

Getting turned on just thinkin' bout it . . .

This particular class we were observing was mostly made up of younger teachers (some of whom were prominent in their own right) all wanting to learn from the "master". There was something special in the way Mattox conducted himself. His very presence demanded attention and respect. All eyes were glued to him. (The only other person I've ever seen have this affect on people was our Steven Peck.) If there's one thing that turns me on more than any other (I'm getting excited just thinking about it), it's excellence . . . and, it was excellence we were most definitely witnessing.

Usually at this kind of convention, the instructor will teach the material they've come prepared to give and not get overly concerned if some, or many, of the students don't fully understand what it is they're trying to get across. I'm not saying the teacher doesn't care, it's just that the classes are one-time events that really don't allow enough time to delve deeply into the true essence of one's technique. As we watched him teach, we could see he was getting annoyed at some of the students. We were actually pleased to see he cared enough to get annoyed.

We sat spellbound as we watched him perform the movements, port de bras, and classic jazz positions in such a way that is rarely seen these days. It was as if we were watching some kind of historical film, except he was right there, live. It was also fascinating to see him get frustrated over the same kinds of things that frustrate us. He was explaining how this particular jazz position, as well as the arm and shoulder isolation associated with it, was to be executed. Just as any real educator would do, he was also explaining the essence, or internal (emotional) feeling, that must exist to not only accompany the movement/step, but also to generate it. The understanding of what part of the body generates or initiates a movement, step or position, along with the right "feel", changes the very way it's executed and, subsequently, looks.

That's where so many young, and unfortunately not so young, dancers fall short. For the inexperienced dancer, movements are mostly mechanical in nature. That's okay, that's how everyone starts, with the basic mechanics. This class, however, was not made up of beginners. Remember, they were mostly teachers and it was one particular teacher (one of those supposedly respected in her own right) that he zeroed in on. She was clearly not a beginning dancer or teacher, and someone who he thought should be able to understand the meaning behind as well as the actual execution of the movements. In frustration, Mattox got down off the platform he was on and made his way over to her and began to physically move her limbs about trying to get her to understand what he wanted. As much as he tried, though, she just wasn't getting it.

Matt Mattox had come from excellence—the very best that Musical Theater/ Jazz ever produced. His teaching philosophy obviously carried with it a passion and dedication to imparting that excellence to future generations. If these teachers could not understand what, why, and how something was to be performed, then, Heaven help us, how would future generations of dancers ever understand? It was so very obvious that for him teaching dance wasn't just a job that allowed him to continue earning money in his later years. No sir, for him, it was a major responsibility for which he did not take lightly.

After his class was finished, we went up and introduced ourselves. He was gracious enough to give us some time and we had a nice talk. As I said before, I was anxious to get his first hand-opinion so I asked him point blank: "What was Jack Cole like to work with?" His answer was pretty much what I expected: "He could be a son of a bitch, a real taskmaster; you loved him or you hated him". He also threw in, "He was a genius". Pretty cool, huh? It was almost verbatim what I heard from others about other early Musical Theater giants such as Jerome Robbins, Bob Fosse, and the one I got to work for, Michael Kidd. In 2013 the dance world lost an iconic figure when Mattox passed away at the age of 91.

All these men were highly regarded -- even thought of as geniuses -- for their exceptional contribution to the theatrical world by audiences, critics, and the very people that worked for them. They were, without exception, real taskmasters. For many, you either loved them or hated them. Truth be told, many dancers both loved and hated them.

The good, the nice, and the ugly . . .

Students tend to like teachers who fall into the "nice" category, meaning easygoing, soft-spoken and nurturing—you know, the kind that treats you like you're five years old. That's fine if you're five years old, though I'd still argue for someone who insists his or her students, no matter what age, work to their maximum capacity. It's certainly understandable why someone would want to study with someone who's "nice". After all, who wants to take a class from a meanie? Meanies are bad! Or are they? Well, that's part of what I want to get into in this chapter.

"Nice doesn't mean good!" (Dennonism #25) Nice is a very nice word that means only one thing—it means nice! I'm not saying that an instructor needs to be mean, as in physically or emotionally abusive, in order to be good, but what is often mistaken for mean is generally a high degree of <u>passion</u>, <u>intensity</u> and <u>integrity</u> and, in some cases (as with Cole, Mattox, Robbins, Fosse, and Kidd), genius. (You may need to refer back to Chapter One, "What Is Art and Who Are Artists".)

In no way do I mean to suggest that we belong in that category, mind you, but Sayhber and I have often been misinterpreted as being "mean". As a matter of fact, on more than one occasion while in the ladies room (apparently a lot of interesting conversations go on in there), Sayhber has overheard a student (no doubt someone who suffers from the "Princess Syndrome") referring to her as the "B" word. I've overheard some pretty harsh comments made about me as well. What these students have done is mistaken our integrity, our unwavering commitment to excellence, along with our fiery passion as being harsh and, yes, even mean.

The reactions of these students lead me to believe that we may be the very first teachers they've come across that have attempted to treat them like grown-ups by challenging them to work beyond their complacent, mediocre level. They've no doubt been brought up to equate nice with good, and intense or strong with mean and downright ugly. It's not just students who believe this either. Many instructors have bought into the idea that their teaching methods should always be packaged in kindergarten-style "nice", so as not to hurt anyone's feelings. Personally, it drives me nuts to hear grown-up teachers talking to college-age students as if they're still infants. How are these young ones going to be ready for real life if they're continually treated like children?

The very best teachers, choreographers and directors I've ever sat, stood, and danced under have been strong, dynamic, and extremely intense artists. These are the people I learned the most from. For someone whose feelings have been placed ahead of actual learning, these teachers could be thought of as being mean, but if one looks closer and deeper, one can see that they are extraordinarily passionate, artistic people who genuinely care about what they are doing and are genuinely concerned with their students' growth, both as artists and people. Now, I ask you, who are you going to learn the most from, the nice, sweet Mr. Rogers type person who allows for mediocrity and complacency, all under the guise of not offending, or the perceived "mean" guy who pushes you beyond your self-imposed limits to greater heights than you thought possible?

Nature, nurture, or training? . . .

In Chapter Six, we discussed the ten qualities or "keys" that make for the proverbial excellent work ethic. In Chapter Seven, we talked about self-leadership, which is the "master key" that puts it all into operation. The question becomes, are *those precious, exceptional, excellent few* (those who operate far above the norm) born with some kind of excellence gene that impels them to work the way they do, or are their parents, guardians, and/or teachers to be credited with instilling the qualities and attributes that make for success? It's the same old question—nature or nurture?

Personally, I don't like the word nurture, because it suggests a kind of "mothering". I prefer a more adult way of dealing with students. My way is more of "demanding". Don't get me wrong, there is a time and place for nurturing—usually with young children, the elderly, those with learning disabilities, and possibly those who are going through or have just emerged from some traumatic experience. For the vast majority of us, however, nurturing can actually stifle. That's my opinion, and I'm sticking to it.

Putting "nurturing" aside, for me, the question is better posed this way: Is it nature or training? The answer is a resounding yes! Yes, nature (meaning one's innate talent) is very important, but, training (meaning work) is even more important. (Re-read Chapter 5, "Four Factors That Determine Success", for all the particulars.) As far as I'm concerned, the reason one excels at anything, be it athletic, artistic, or academic, centers on a concept that every world-class athlete of any sport knows from years of experience. It's called "training", and that means work!

Yes, we're all born with certain talents, but those talents lie completely dormant until they've been identified and worked. It's unfortunate, but true; human nature generally leads one to operate at a primitive, base level—that of doing the least one can in order to survive. That's where the teacher/trainer, coach/trainer, parent/trainer comes into play. Here's the thing . . .

THiNG # 26

iT HAS TO BE TAUGHT! THEY HAVE TO BE TRAiNED!

The skills necessary to operate in the realm of excellence do not come easily, let alone, naturally. They have to be taught, and then instilled, which means worked over and over again. Teachers often confuse teaching with training. Teaching means imparting knowledge. Training means to work over and over again. In the theater, it's called rehearsing.

This is where I believe many teachers (also managers and, yes, even parents) have failed our youth. They give lip service to the idea of excellence, but do little to actually instill (that means train) the excellence attributes. It's not enough to occasionally mention that everyone should work hard and do their best. What students need is a detailed explanation of what it means to operate in an excellent manner and why it is in their best interest to do so. Then, like a trainer preparing an athlete for the Olympics, teachers (also managers and, yes, parents) must put their charges on a training regimen to practice the desired skills until they become deeply entrenched.

Students would be better served from an early age, if they were in a constant state of training in the ways of excellence.

Excellence does not mean perfection . . .

Lest anyone misunderstand what I'm saying, I'm not advocating perfection. Excellence and perfection are two different things. Excellence has as much to do with one's approach and effort, as it has to do with any eventual outcome, and the outcome I'm referring to has mainly to do with reaching ones own maximum potential.

It's been said that an excellent effort will produce excellent results, but that does not mean the excellent results can be considered perfection. That's because we're all born with different talents and gifts, which also impact one's achievements or results. Two people can work equally hard for the same length of time attempting to learn the same thing but, because of their respective innate, God-given talent, one will likely do better. If one ends up better than the other, how can they both be credited with reaching perfection? They can't -- neither of them can -- but they could both be credited with achieving a certain level of excellence.

The truth is, no matter how good a person gets at doing something, he or she can never be thought of as having reached perfection. To achieve perfection is to have reached the mountaintop, meaning you can't go any higher. Perfection pre-supposes there can be no more improvement. A lot of people may think that way, but real artists (actually, anyone who constantly strives for excellence) never believe they've reached a state of perfection. I put it this way: **"Perfection doesn't really exist, except as a metaphorical reference point to work towards!" (Dennonism #26)**

If perfection doesn't exist, what about the oft-used adage, "practice makes perfect"? In 1981, we came across an article in Dance Magazine excerpted from a book entitled, *A Guide to the Dancer You can Be*, by Ellen Jacob, where she had altered the saying to become what I believe is a much more effective teaching tool. Here's the thing . . .

THiNG # 27

PRACTiCE MAKES . . . PERMANENT!

Practice (training) can certainly make better, but it can also make worse. What if you practiced (trained) incorrectly? What practice really does is firmly fix or establish a physical, mental, or behavioral skill. In other words, it makes permanent!

That's why it's so important to have an excellent instructor. It's the instructor's job to see to it that the student doesn't practice incorrectly. So, let's get at the true meaning of practice, i.e. training.

• • DEFiNiTiON TiME • •

Practicing is the act of application—meaning an ongoing, daily, habitual execution of a desired skill until it becomes deeply engrained to the point of seeming almost "natural". It's not just thinking or theorizing about something, but actually physically doing. I put it this way: **"The secret to learning anything is repetition, repetition, repetition . . . and then repeat!" (Dennonism #27)**

We've all used the phrase: "It's been drilled into me". That means that something has been forever embedded in our brains and/or bodies and we couldn't forget it if we tried. Drilling is training through repetition. We're back to where I believe many teachers fail their students. Sure, they'll mention an important point, or have the class recite something once or twice, or they tell the class to review the material "as needed". Then the child goes home and when asked by his or her parent: "What'd you learn today", the answer is: "I dunno". They don't know because whatever material was covered that day wasn't really drilled into them. The material was barely laid on top of their brains. Whatever information the teacher was attempting to impart gets blown away by more pressing needs like texting, tweeting, or Instagram.

This is something educator Jamie Escalante understood so very well. He drilled his math students by having them repeat math formulas over and over and over again. He would line them up and make a game out of it. If someone missed, they went to the back of the line. He understood that math problems could only be solved if you knew and understood the formula that gets you there. He understood this very important truth—only through drilling (constant repetition) does someone really learn and retain or, as Steven Peck would say: **"You gotta own it!" (Steven's saying #8)**

10,000 hours to excellence . . .

In the book *Outliers*, author Malcolm Gladwell discusses something called the 10,000-Hour Rule. He explains how in the early 1990s, Swedish psychologist Dr. K. Anders Ericsson experimented by dividing violin students into three groups. The first group contained those ". . . with the potential to become world-class soloists." These were the ones who'd no doubt become professionals. The second group contained " . . . those judged to be merely "good." The third group contained those who were "unlikely to ever play professionally and who intended to become music teachers in the public school system".

Through a series of questions it was determined that the reason each student fell into one of these three categories -- world-class soloist, "good", music teacher -- had more to do with how many hours they practiced than with "innate talent". As Gladwell writes, " . . . he and his colleagues couldn't find any 'naturals', musicians who floated effortlessly to the top while practicing a fraction of the time their peers did. Nor could they find any 'grinds', meaning people who worked harder than anyone else, yet didn't have what it takes to break the top ranks". It was determined that by age twenty, the music teacher group put in only four thousand hours, the "good" group put in eight thousand hours and the first group, those most likely to become "world-class soloists", had put in 10,000 hours. The basic conclusion was that the better musicians were better because they put in more time than their counterparts.

The same could be said for those who dance. It's no secret why those who make it in the professional world of dance do so—they put in the requisite "10,000 hours" of practice. As Gretchen Ward Warren says in her book, *Classical Ballet Technique*: "It takes approximately eight years of attending classes, usually begun at the age of nine or ten, to produce a dancer of professional-level competency." My experience as a professional dancer and teacher bears that out. I would add one other thing to what she said. The "professional-level competency" one reaches after eight or so years of practice is only the beginning. Dancers, like musicians, like all artists, are continually striving to improve their capabilities. Their initial 10,000 hours soon becomes 15, 000, then 20,000, and more!

Matters of character begin with respect . . .

I've made the case that both physical and mental skills not only need to be taught, they need to be intensely drilled, but what about matters of character? To me it's a no-brainer that when dealing with matters of "excellence", one is ultimately dealing with matters of character, and when dealing with matters of character, one is ultimately dealing with matters of Key # 10, RESPECT.

Every so often, I'll need to point out that a few of my students are not exercising any self-leadership skills by centering their attention on me when I'm speaking and demonstrating. Not only does that impede their learning, but they are also showing disrespect for me, the classroom, their fellow students, the subject matter, the school, and I could go on and on. That leads me to ask: "How come the good dancers are always listening and doing their best to implement my instructions and the bad dancers are completely oblivious?"

That leads me to the broader and more philosophical question: **"Are the good, good because they listen, or do they listen because they're good?" (Dennonism #28)** Ultimately the answer doesn't really matter because, either way, they're both listening and good!

In our collective 80-plus years of teaching, we've noticed a discernable degradation of etiquette and protocol that has resulted in what I call: **"A generation of respect/responsibility illiterates!" (Dennonism #29)** What's being tolerated today has led to a growing number of workers/students who do not know how to properly conduct themselves in a workplace environment.

Fostering an air of reverence . . .

An educator knows how to create an environment of excellence (where learning happens at an accelerated rate) by fostering an air of reverence. Aretha Franklin had it right when she sang, R – E – S – P – E – C – T . . . sock it to me, sock it to me!

An example where the teaching of respect produces an accelerated rate of learning is found in an educational program highlighted in *Outliers*, called KIPP (Knowledge Is Power Program). It began as an experimental program in the mid 1990s and, as of this writing, has grown into over 100 KIPP schools (elementary, middle, and high schools) in 20 states and the District of Columbia. More than 85 percent of their students are from low-income families and 95 percent are African American or Latino. Their success rate is spectacular. Nationally, more than 95 percent of KIPP middle school students have graduated high school, and more than 85 percent of KIPP alumni have gone on to college.

So where does the respect thing come in? As Gladwell states in his book, "In the classroom they are taught to turn and address anyone talking to them in a protocol known as "SSLANT": Smile, Sit Up, Listen, Ask Questions, Nod when being spoken to, and Track with your eyes." Do you see the connection between how they are being *trained* to behave and their eventual success? The code of behavior they are to adhere to in the classroom fosters an air of reverence, which in turn produces an environment of excellence, which then hastens positive results.

Jaimie Escalante, John Wooden, Jack Cole, Jerome Robbins, Michael Kidd, Matt Mattox, and our Steven Peck are all examples of educators (instructors whose teachings transcend the subject matter) who would never tolerate disrespect.

There's one other person I'd like to include. On February 18, 2011, basketball Hall of Fame inductee Bill Russell was interviewed on CNN's John King about his being awarded the Presidential Medal of Honor, and I found what he said so beautifully expressed. When asked why he thought he was chosen for, or deserved, the Presidential Medal of Freedom, he said: "When I played for the Boston Celtics, especially after I became the captain, I considered myself sort of a big brother to my teammates . . . and I always acted the same way to my community. I tried to make sure that I and my friends were always treated with respect . . . and I used to always say, whether anyone likes me or not is irrelevant. The relevant thing to me was to be respected, and by being respected myself, and being respectful, it can create an atmosphere that the folks . . . they could see the folks around me are also people to be respected."

Isn't that beautiful? He encapsulated in those few sentences something that every real educator understands: that caring whether you're liked or not is irrelevant, and even counter-productive; and, that insisting on and requiring respect from those in our charge is key to creating an "atmosphere" (important word) that, in turn, perpetuates more respect, which doesn't just allow for, but hastens, positive results, which in Bill Russell's case was a magnificent career with many championship seasons.

Whenever I hear a professional coach of any sport being interviewed, they'll eventually get around to saying that the key to their success is they "expect" nothing but the best from their players. That "expecting" nothing but the best means they will accept nothing less, which brings us right back to their demanding the very best.

Another one of coach John Wooden's famous quotes speaks to this very point: "For me it is never simply a case of win or lose, because I do not demand victory. What I demand (and that's exactly the word) is that each player expend every available ounce of energy to achieve his personal best, to attain competitive greatness as I define it."

Rules, protocols, and standards . . .

Real educators don't just make polite Mr. Rogers type requests or suggestions and then hope for the best. They demand one's very best efforts and settle for nothing less. It's basically a three-pronged strategy:

1) Impose   2) Demand   3) Hold Accountable.

I've known many instructors who don't like to impose too many, if any, rules or regulations. They like a freer, less stringent atmosphere—a kind of Isadora Duncan approach. It is my contention that we do our students a disservice by not imposing strict rules. The hardcore fact is that, no matter what one does in life and no matter where one does it, there are going to be some set of rules and/or protocols that are required of him or her.

That means they will have to be able to live up to a pre-determined set of rules and standards whether they like them or not. Get that . . . whether they like them or not! So when I'm asked why so many rules, or why any rules, I respond with the most important answer first. Here's the thing . . .

THiNG # 28

THE PRiMARY REASON FOR HAViNG RULES AND SETTiNG HiGH STANDARDS iS SO STUDENTS BECOME WELL-SKiLLED iN FOLLOWiNG RULES AND STRiViNG TO ACHiEVE HiGH STANDARDS!

Setting high standards serves to stretch one's character "muscles". It almost doesn't matter what the rules and standards are. What's important is the act of striving for or reaching to obtain an imposed or expected high level, or standard, of behavior.

Getting back to the military analogy, the drill sergeant doesn't put a second's thought into whether or not the new recruit likes him or her. He's out to transform what is essentially raw material into something greater than the recruit ever thought possible. He knows what they don't—that what he is teaching and training them could one day save their life, not to mention the rest of us. At first, the new recruits think the sergeant is a madman whose only desire in life is to impose pain and suffering. For the sergeant (and me) that's just a byproduct of his or her job . . . a perk, if you will.

After a period of time, the recruit will begin to understand that all of what he or she is being forced (that's the demanding, insisting thing) to do and learn is for his or her own benefit. As far as I'm concerned, school is a form of boot camp. It's a time of preparation for the battles of life, which begins in earnest after graduation. So, what's the moral of the story? Give a "meanie" a chance!

Setting the tone . . .

So, how exactly does one teach discipline, focus, responsibility, energy, or any of the values *those precious, exceptional, excellent few* possess?

For me, it starts with the very first meeting. Whenever I enter a workplace environment I don't just expect respect, I demand it. That means until each student stops what he or she is doing and turns his or her attention towards me I will not proceed. When first I step to the front of the class, I wait to see how the students respond. Generally those who've been in my class before turn their attention to me demonstrating they are aware of my presence and understand their attention (focus) is required.

With some exceptions, those who are new to me remain steeped in conversation with friends, often with their backs to me. This, of course, is a sure sign of ignorance (for which they need to be taught) and, of course, disrespect (for which they need to be trained). After a short time, I address the class and ask in my kindest, most Mr. Rogers way for their attention. This is how I know that being Mr. Rogers-like in one's demeanor doesn't really work, for at best, it gets maybe a few more to acknowledge me. Sadly, there are still others who remain completely oblivious to my presence.

I then raise the intensity of my voice and ask again. This gets more to notice me, but there are always, yes I'm afraid always, those who need "special" encouragement. Here's where I make my stand, both literally and metaphorically. I wait intently (there's power in stillness) till eventually those who have quieted down take it upon themselves to silence the others. It matters not whether it takes 10 seconds or 10 minutes, I wait.

Not only do I insist on silence, I have everyone turn their entire bodies, not just their heads, toward me. I then say "good morning". I'm usually met with a half-hearted response. I say it again. Most of the class will respond, but that's not good enough. I instruct the class that they all must participate and that the energy they chose to put into their response indicates the energy they've decided to put into their learning. So I say "good morning" again. If I notice someone didn't respond with the rest of the class, I point right at him or her and say you didn't participate, let's try it again. Usually, at this point, everyone responds. When I finally get a focused, energetic response from everyone, I respond with "excellent, now we can proceed".

The class has just received lessons number one and two: Their attention is required before class proceeds -- before I will proceed -- and they must all participate— slackers will not be tolerated! At that very moment, our very first meeting, I'm setting the tone of the class as well as making clear what I expect (a form of demanding) from them in terms of listening and responding, which is, of course, a respectful thing to do. At this very first meeting, I've begun the training process in how I want them to behave. In other words, I'm cultivating an "air of reverence" by insisting that they be respecful.

It's amazing to see how many of these: **"Poor unfortunates!" (Steven's saying #9)** look at me as if I'm the rude one for interrupting their conversations. Their bewildered looks reveal that this may be the very first time they've ever been asked (or should I say made) to stop, silence themselves, turn to face the instructor, and respond. It must be the first time, or they wouldn't look so befuddled.

The principal benefit of a respectful, attentive attitude is that it sets the mind to better receive. Teachers who do not teach, demand, and continually train students in respect are doing the students, themselves, all other teachers (present and future), as well as all of society, a disservice. Creating an "atmosphere of excellence" necessitates an "air of reverence".

Students need to realize that without their respect, a teacher will not be able to put 100% of his or her effort into his or her teaching. Every student suffers from the few (or more) of other students who do not put forth a respectful attitude. It's best for those students who do wish to be there to have those who do not wish to be there either mature up or "exit stage left"!

Another important reason for having a respectful learning environment is so those students who are of a shyer, more timid nature will feel secure and safe enough (who say's I'm not nurturing?) to fully participate. Too often, the unruly, disrespectful few dominate the proceedings. I know, because that's how it was for me when I was in school, and that's how it was for my children. I also see it in every class I teach. The shyer ones are reluctant to get involved when the instructor doesn't require restraint, i.e. respect, from those who are blessed with little or no inhibitions.

Allowing is just another word for teaching . . .

Often, the problem I find with some instructors is not in what they teach, is not what they advocate, it's in what they allow. Let me give you a few examples.

Example #1: BAD!

Some time ago, I passed by the door of the dance studio in one of the colleges where I teach and watched as the instructor took roll. I was distressed to see that as she took roll, nary a student was paying any attention. My first thought was how disrespectful her students were being. My second thought was why was she allowing them to be so disrespectful? My third thought was, no wonder so many students look at Sayhber and me as if we're nuts . . . we must be the only teachers that require students to be attentive and responsive!

Example #2: BADDER!!

At another college where I teach there is this long walk from one side of the campus, where I pick up my mail, to the other side where my class is held. Along my walk I'll peek into the many classrooms I pass to check out the "atmosphere". You don't have to hear what's being said to know what's going on. Often, I see the instructor at a podium up front pontificating his or her little heart out to a group of students whose body language screams disinterest, i.e. disrespect. Many are slouched as if napping, some are turned toward each other, while others are busy playing with their electronic devises. The same three thoughts come to mind—*how, why, and no wonder.*

Example #3: BADDEST!!!

One other time, Sayhber and I arrived a bit early to teach, and we came upon another dance instructor finishing up her class. She was speaking to her students attempting to give them some important information. Most of her students were sitting on the floor while this one gentleman was lying down with his arms covering his face. None of them seemed very interested in what the instructor was saying. The attitude of the class was so obviously disrespectful (to the teacher, the classroom, the institution, to the very concept of learning itself) that both Sayhber and I looked at each other and winced. The same three thoughts came to mind—*how, why, and no wonder.*

This instructor noticed our presence and sensed our uneasiness (it was hard to hold back) at the scene before us so she put forth a rather lame, half-hearted attempt to bring them to attention. She was pretty much ignored. We sensed she feared losing her "friendship" status with the class when she did nothing further to address this blatant lack of respect. At this point, Sayhber (bless her ever-loving drill sergeant heart) couldn't stand it any longer and blurted out in a manner that could not be confused with anything but an order: "Sit up and pay attention, your teacher is talking to you!" Believe me when I say, there is no ignoring Sayhber when she commands something.

Those lazy, disrespectful students perked up as if dynamite had exploded in their underpants. They didn't like being ordered about, but they responded and that's what was important. Sayhber didn't make any friends from that group, but she did demonstrate her unwillingness to allow disrespect in her or the instructor's presence. She may have overstepped her bounds, but the class was now giving the attention and respect that the instructor deserved.

All of these instructors I've described may be knowledgeable in their subject matter, but they know little about the importance of teaching and training (which is even more important) their charges to focus, which of course is the most important aspect of showing respect. Believe me, even if I were to teach an academic class (one where everyone sits at a desk) my methods would not alter. Before I'd utter a single word about the actual subject at hand, I'd make sure everyone's attention was directed toward their teacher. It's not just for me that I would do this—it's for them!

In the corporate/business world, these students wouldn't last a moment allowing their attention to be anywhere other than on their manager when he or she is speaking. I don't care that the students may think me to be "mean", or an old fogey. I know better than they. I'm thinking of their futures—that's a place I've been, and something they need to prepare for.

Daily dose of respect . . .

We talked about the KIPP schools—now let me now give you another example of a place where I experienced respect being taught daily. For many years I taught at a performing arts center in Van Nuys, CA. I had an advanced jazz class, which contained aspiring professionals. This particular studio runs a reputable program that requires a lot from all of its students. To put it bluntly, it imposes many rules and regulations that are designed principally to breed excellence. The school had a scholarship program for very serious, young adult students who desired a career in dance. These students had to sign a contract to commit to a certain length of time. Their commitment included working in and around the studio whenever they weren't in class. That meant attending to the front desk, cleaning the studios and bathrooms, and helping the directors in anyway they could.

These students were required (which means trained) to speak respectfully to everyone, especially the instructors. If they were going to miss a class, they had to write a note to the teacher explaining the situation. If the student was legitimately late for a class, they were to stand just inside the door until the instructor gave permission to join the class. If he or she needed to leave class for any reason, they were to ask -- yes, ask, and not tell -- for permission to do so. At the end of class they were required to walk up to the instructor, shake hands, and express their gratitude.

Please understand, they were required to do these things whether they felt like it or not, or lose their privileges. Their feelings were irrelevant to what was and is considered appropriate behavior. They were in training, not just to become excellent dancers, but also to become excellent, respectful, students which, of course, leads them to become mature, respectful people. Because of the protocols these scholarship students were required to follow, the studio reeked with reverence . . . and because of the "air of reverence" that permeated the place, learning could and did flourish.

I've taught at many other studios, big and small, over the years where, at times, a respectful attitude was hard to find. There was "attitude" all right, but believe me, it wasn't respectful. Disrespect is never warranted, but disrespect from students who are receiving free classes is even worse. Whenever confronted with this kind of situation, the same thoughts come to mind—how disrespectful of these students . . . why are they being allowed to be so, and . . . no wonder they look at us as if we're nuts.

If an instructor, or manager, or parent lets sub-standard behaviors go unchecked, he or she is part of the problem.
Here's the thing . . .

THiNG # 29

ALLOWiNG iS THE SAME AS TEACHiNG!

That which you allow, you have condoned. Condoning means acceptance, which suggests agreement. If a student's disrespectful behavior goes unchallenged, the student is led to believe that it's okay to be disrespectful, which is the same as teaching them to be disrespectful. It's a form of passive instruction.

NEWSFLASH! People (especially young people) will do and get away with what they're allowed to do! As you may surmise, I place a lot of the blame for a student's inability to be respectful on all their previous teachers, including the parents. After all, can you blame a 17-, 18-, or 19-year-old for not knowing how to behave respectfully and responsibly if they've been allowed to be and do otherwise their entire lives? It's time to turn back to basics with tried and true methods -- ones that educators Jaime Escalante and John Wooden used -- by setting high standards of behavior for our students to adhere to, and insisting that they do so.

Finding a reputable school . . .

In a previous chapter, I mentioned how difficult it can be to find a reputable dance class or school, especially if you don't know what to look for. Let me share with you what Sayhber and I looked for when deciding on a dance studio for our daughter, Jessica. We looked for a place with reputation, structure, integrity, standards, discipline, and respect. These were and are the qualities I look for when determining if a school operates in the realm of excellence. Once again they are:

1. Reputation   2. Structure   3. Integrity
4. Standards   5. Discipline   6. Respect

Being dancers ourselves, we knew the value of hard work and discipline, and we knew that there is no better way to instill these qualities than a good dance class. We also knew that our daughter was shy and needed a structured environment to thrive.

One of the places where I was teaching at the time was a dance studio in Chatsworth, CA. No longer in existence, The Rozann-Zimmerman Ballet Center (RZBC) was well known for having several of its students becoming professionals **(reputation)**. One of them, Arianna Lallone, became a principal ballerina with Pacific Northwest Ballet. She began taking my class when she was 12. Even at that age she was showing great promise because of her amazing passion and respect for dance. As a matter of fact, she's one of *those precious, exceptional, excellent few* we continually refer to.

RZBC had a program that set it apart from the majority of local dance studios. Right away, I knew this was a good place to be. It had a graded system (**structure**), whereby each student had certain requirements to fulfill in order to be a part of the program, and its training resulted in producing professional dancers.

The second reason I knew it was probably a good studio was because the owner/director at the time, Chris Shenks, informed us that Jessica was too young to begin. Unlike most neighborhood dance studios, where they'll start kids doing Ballet at too young an age, and then put them on pointe way before they're ready, this studio would not accept a child into their program before he or she was seven, or very close to it (**integrity**), and not put them on pointe until they were ready.

A reputable Ballet program will not take what I call the babies—those under six. Why? Because they are not yet ready to step into a serious, structured program (**standards**) doing something that requires at least an elementary ability to focus and comprehend. A serious dance program (which excludes most neighborhood studios) requires a serious student. When a director of a school turns down business in order to protect the integrity of the school, as well as to uphold standards, that's something!

Our daughter's very first class at RZBC convinced me more than ever that she was in the right place. The students were required to stand at attention (**discipline**) in first position (heels together, feet turned out) with their hands behind their backs facing the teacher (**respect**) before and after each exercise at the barre. Her teacher, the most excellent Miss Carrie, a strong yet quiet person, fostered an "air of reverence" by teaching and training these young first-timers how to be still, which is, of course, another important aspect of respect.

Our Jessica learned at age seven what we find lacking in many of our college-age students. Students of all ages, in all classes, in all subjects should be continually taught the value of stillness—the value of a quiet, focused mind.

Please understand, the purpose of quiet and stillness isn't just to keep the noise down. Being quiet isn't a time for the brain to shut down. Here's the thing . . .

THING # 30

THERE'S POWER IN SILENCE AND STILLNESS!

Silence and stillness, when used purposefully, can be a wonderful tool that helps one to process information that's been directed toward him or her. Silence and stillness allows for focusing, which gives opportunity for the mind to explore the full relevance and value of what's being taught.

Too many young ones (and yes, not so young ones) are ill at ease when confronted with silence. They see it as some kind of awkward, mysterious void that needs to be filled. On occasion, I've said something that I believe to be essential -- maybe even profound (it can happen) -- only to have its significance completely missed because a student, or two, or three, thought it necessary to begin speaking as soon as -- sometimes almost before -- I finished. The need to immediately respond acts as a kind of repellent that keeps the brain from receiving the full value of what has been said.

Like all techniques, the technique of being still and silent, along with it's necessary companion contemplation, has to be taught and, once again, that brings us right back to what our job as an educator is—to help our students learn how to learn, grow, and mature.

So, before deciding upon a dance school for yourself, or your child, it's best to go and observe some classes. "Yea great, but I don't know enough to know what to look for". Not to worry—here's what I tell my students to look for when determining if a class, or teacher is good. It's very simple, really. If you see as many different versions of any given position, step, or movement pattern, as there are students, something is wrong. An instructor with integrity will be quite insistent that each student be working toward the same goal. That goal is the understanding of, and the proper execution of, a clearly defined set of techniques. Basically that means, however many students there are in the room, they'll each look as closely like the others as possible. In other words, the same technique ought to produce the same appearance.

I'm not talking about students becoming mindless robots—I'm talking about their executing every position, step, and movement pattern precisely as the teacher has demonstrated. After all, there is only one teacher presumably demonstrating what he or she wants in only one, certain way.

As I teach my students: **"The correct arm, or leg, or body position at any given time, is the one that is set!" (Dennonism #30)** This simply means that whatever the instructor demonstrates or asks for becomes, at that very moment, the only way to do it. It doesn't mean that the given step, position, or movement pattern can't be performed numerous other ways, it just means that the instructor has determined how he or she wants it and, at that moment in time, that's how it should be performed.

If a teacher allows everyone to do his or her own "thing", that probably means the instructor doesn't have a precise technique he or she is trying to convey. It also means his or her standards are low. That's not good. Instructors with high standards don't allow for deviation. They insist (that's that demanding thing again) that their students work up to those high standards. The bottom line is, unless you're observing an improvisation class where students are exploring alternative ways of moving, the more alike the students look, the better the teacher.

It's also a good idea to speak directly to the head of the school, and to the prospective teacher. Ask them about their philosophy concerning dance and teaching. You can also check out their website and, if possible, attend one of their recitals. But most importantly when observing a class, whether you have any real knowledge of dance or not, you can still see and sense the level of respect in the classroom.

So, once again, my criteria for determining if a school, teacher, and class falls into the excellent category are:

1. **Reputation**   2. **Structure**   3. **Integrity**
4. **Standards**   5. **Discipline**   6. **Respect**

It all boils down to the "atmosphere". Did you notice, I didn't mention anything about having fun? Okay, if fun is what you want, then is everybody laughing hysterically throughout the class?

"You're not gonna make it" . . .

Our son, Matthew, began Tae Kwon Do at age seven. Boy, if you want to see an "air of reverence", check out your local Martial Arts Academy. The very first thing he learned to do was to bow before entering the room. He then would have to bow before entering the work area. He and fellow classmates would bow many times over to the instructor and to each other all throughout the class. They would bow when class was finished, and would then bow again before exiting the premises.

The instructor, a South Korean black belt many times over, would often admonish the kids to concentrate and work very hard or, as he put it: "You're not gonna make it". That was his cryptic way of saying that their progress and moving up the ladder, or belt, of success depended on being attentive and working very, very hard. I found it fascinating that all these young kids were learning how to show respect before, during, and after any of the actual martial art techniques.

Matt went on to earn his black belt, and continued doing other forms of Martial Arts for several more years. Of all the things our son learned doing Martial Arts (discipline, focusing, hard work, beating each other senseless), the most important as far as his mother and I are concerned, was respect. We who instruct in other areas, be it academic, athletic or artistic, could learn a lot from our Martial Arts brethren—respect first, learning second.

That brings me to another one of my favorite quotes from teacher/coach/writer/educator John Wooden: "Practice is where champions are created". Coach Wooden had his players working full out in all his practice sessions. The practice session was never to be undervalued by being disrespected.

There's a saying we've been using for many years now. We got it from that sultry, long-legged dancer/actress/choreographer Ann Reinking, who most likely got it from her mentor, musical theater icon, Bob Fosse.

Here's the thing . . .

THiNG # 31

PRACTICE YOUR PERFORMANCE!

The quality of one's performance is directly related to the quality of one's practice. You cannot "mark" your rehearsal and expect to perform brilliantly. A half-hearted effort brings only mediocre results. You'll only perform as well as you practice.

Learning skills such as focusing, being energetic, stoking passion, acting responsibly, looking intelligent and every other "key" that makes for excellence -- which of course all lead up to the primary key of respect -- are all acquired by means of practice. It takes practice . . . it takes training!

A rose by any other name still smells . . .

This brings me to another important concept that needs to be taught, that of earned rewards. I don't like the concept of punishment because it makes it sound as if a person is being . . . "punished". The phrase I prefer to use is "earned reward". That means that wherever a student finds him or herself, good or bad, first or last, is a place they themselves have worked to be.

Keep in mind, I don't count the winnings one may obtain from gambling, nor do I count "participation trophies" or what all too often happens in our public school system, something called "social promotion" where students are promoted to the next grade level, not because they've earned it, but because so called "educators" don't wish to bruise the poor child's self-esteem. You know what I think about the self-indulgent self-esteem movement.

What I teach is that each individual is responsible for whatever successes they achieve. Now, I'm not so dumb as to not know that, on occasion, a person's promotion or position in a given workplace may have been heavily influenced by circumstances that have little to do with being earned. Can we all say nepotism, favoritism, or discrimination? Setting those things aside, generally: **"9 times out of 7" (Dennonism # 31)**, a person's achievements, or lack thereof, are the result of what that person has worked for.

Here's the thing . . .

THiNG # 32

WHERE YOU ARE TODAY iS A RESULT OF WHAT YOU DiD YESTERDAY!

For the most part, your position in life, in school, on a team, or at the workplace is the result of what you've done up to that point. It's where you deserve to be by virtue of the work, or lack thereof, you've put in. So too, the knowledge you possess is a result of the work you've put in.

Notice that nothing comes without first putting in the work! We're back to understanding that the work one puts in is an investment (Key # 3) toward one's future. Please understand, where you'll be tomorrow will be a result of what you do today, so get on the floor and get to work!

In my thinking, a person who is sentenced to jail time isn't being punished. He's being rewarded for the work he's performed. If a person gets a speeding ticket that costs him or her several hundreds of dollars, it's not punishment, they are simply being rewarded for having a lead foot. I know I'm playing with words, but thinking this way places the credit (let's not use the word blame) on the individual.

If we teach our students to think in terms of earned rewards, they'll better understand that all achievement, whether positive or negative, is something they are responsible for. That's the important lesson here—they are responsible (all things being Kosher) for what they get. It's such an important lesson in and about life. Just as I say to replace the word "esteem" with "respect", replace the word "punishment" with "earned reward". If one of my students complains to me about their grade, I simply tell them I've rewarded them with the grade that they worked so hard to earn. This puts the responsibility where it belongs, on them—congratulations!

Conclusion . . .

It is the instructor's responsibility to set the tone of his or her class, and that tone should be one of respect. It is up to the instructor to implement rules, protocols, and high standards their students must work towards. It is up to the instructor to instill in his or her students attributes that will enable the student to become the best learner he or she can be. Before someone can become a great dancer, singer, actress, athlete, or academic scholar, he or she must understand that it is they who are responsible for their own achievements.

Educators know that the best way to create an environment of excellence (one where everyone is not just encouraged to learn, but pushed, probed and prodded into doing so, and nothing less than excellence of effort is tolerated) is to foster, check that – is to insist on - an "air of reverence". Show me a place where respect abounds (such as the KIPP program with the protocol SSLANT) and I'll show you a place where learning flourishes.

In the next, and yes, you'll no doubt be relieved to know, final chapter, I'm going to get into something for which I often get a lot of flack, both from students and even sometimes from my fellow instructors. I believe it to be another important tool that helps to improve the atmosphere of the learning/working environment. Take a breather, change your outfit if you like, and I'll see you on the next page.

Sayhber teaching mid-1980s
Photo: Judy Francesconi

CHAPTER TEN
THE DREADED DRESS CODE
BOND, JAMES BOND!

"Some bellies ought never be shown; some bellies ought never be seen!" I will never forget the terrific experience I had when I did the Mel Brooks film *History of the World, Part I*. That was the first of two Mel Brooks films I did for director/choreographer Alan Johnson (the other being *Dracula, Dead and Loving It*). The large-scale production number we were doing was a dazzling spoof of the not so funny historical event known as the Inquisition. The whole thing was staged, choreographed, and filmed in the style of the great movie musical spectaculars that Hollywood became famous for in the 1940s and 50s.

Johnson, a three-time Emmy-winning choreographer, cleverly choreographed a terrifically funny song written by Brooks that had the dancers portraying monks and torturers. I had worked for Johnson many times, and I have nothing but praise for his talents, professionalism and, sense of humor. This time out, he cast me as one of the featured torturers—something many of my students might think completely appropriate.

Brooks himself played Torquemada, the Grand Inquisitor, as only someone with his whacky sense of humor could. There we all were, on the Paramount lot for days singing and dancing our little mean-spirited hearts out. Also included in the production was an Esther Williams tribute with nuns disrobing from their Habits, revealing their 1940s style one piece bathing suits, doing a hilarious synchronized swimming routine in an underground pool located right in the sound stage we were using. If you get a moment, YouTube it and you'll see what I mean.

I have to say that spending a few weeks in the presence of a comic genius like Mel Brooks was more than a learning experience. I watched Brooks jump back and forth from performer to director over and over again without missing a beat. I also watched intently as he worked with comic geniuses like Jackie Mason and Ronny Graham (both manacled to a post) in order to get just the right performance out of them. Like all Brooks films, this was a period/spoof piece, which means it's a costume piece, which means you got to wear a whole lot of not-so-comfortable stuff in order to be in the picture.

While working this job I was very much reminded of what every actor learns pretty quickly, which is: when playing a part, it's helpful to dress the part, in order to feel the part, in order to help you become the part. When filming that dance sequence, I spent well over an hour each day getting "made up" and into costume in order to complete the look. I never complained. All actors understand that a large part of getting into character involves the transformation of one's appearance.

In this chapter, I want to explore what I believe to be another very important tool in helping to create an atmosphere of excellence. It's one that is often overlooked.

Dressing the part . . .

One need not be an actor to understand that wearing certain clothing or accessories affects how one feels and acts, not to mention how one is perceived and treated by others. In the business world, there is the concept of "dressing for success". If you want to succeed in the corporate world, you need to begin dressing the part long before anyone hires you. In other words, you need to look successful before you actually are. This goes right along with the concepts of acting professional before you become one and, as I said in Chapter 7, exercising the "leadership of self" before anyone gives you the opportunity to lead others.

As you've no doubt surmised, this chapter is about the ever-controversial dress code. I'm sure there are some of you who will readily agree with me on the concept of a dress code, but you may not be aware of all the practical reasons for doing so. That's what I aim to get across. It is my contention that the implementation of some kind of dress code increases discipline, order, and best of all . . . respect, which all leads to a better learning environment. Read through and, if by the time you finish you don't agree with me, feel free to strip down in protest.

True story time . . .

Once upon a time, a rather dazzling Jazz dance instructor (I'm not saying it was me, although he did have a nicely coiffed beard) walked into class and was astonished by what he saw. It was as if he had been tossed over the rainbow and through the woods only to end up in Never, Never Land. He saw his students dressed in bizarre, peculiar, multi-colored outfits and wearing all kinds of sparkly, mostly cheap, costume jewelry as if they were about to compete in a strangely concocted extraterrestrial fashion show.

If that weren't enough, he could see many had rings on their fingers and, yes, bells on their toes. He noticed hanging, dangling earrings all over the place, and a few even had on display beautiful, decorative belly button rings. Then he couldn't help but notice that many were wearing a style of clothing that seemed to be all the rage, you know, the low, very low-cut pants or shorts -- the kind that fit below the hip bones -- as well as those skimpy, trashy-looking crop tops—you've seen them, the ones that barely cover a person's . . . a person's . . . well let's just say a person.

It was at that point when the proverbial light bulb went off in the instructor's head and he realized that almost nobody was wearing what virtually all dance students in his day did, that which could be considered genuine, authentic dancewear—you know, "wear" made for dancing. It became very clear that the instructor wasn't anywhere near Kansas anymore.

Now, the story is true, except the part about it happening all in one day. Also, the teacher in the story was actually two teachers—me and my partner-in-crime, Sayhber, though I'm fairly sure she wasn't the one with a beard.

Young (and not so young) dancers were increasingly wearing anything and everything to dance class except, ironically, the kind of clothing that is made specifically for dance. On top of that, the jingling, jangling sound of the jewelry, as well as the constant stopping to make adjustments with said jewelry, made it more and more difficult for them and us to concentrate. Then, on top of that top, there were the exposed, bare midriffs we were forced to endure, not to mention -- though I must -- the exposed butt cracks that many young ladies were completely unaware they were exhibiting. That's the problem with the low cut "style"—there's no room for error! It looks silly and reveals a juvenile, childish immaturity that I for one, and Sayhber for two, are doing our best to combat.

Listen, as politically incorrect as this may be, not every "body" is created equal. Don't take offense; I'm doing my best to be discreet here. There are some bellies that are a real pleasure to look at because they're extremely trim and slim, and have all kinds of crisscross lines on them. There are however, bellies that are not so pleasing to look at.

For my own defense, I came up with a saying I've been using in my classes for a long time now: **"Some bellies ought never be shown; some bellies ought never be seen!"** (Dennonism #32) Please don't take offense; I didn't call out your name.

I cannot and will not discriminate in my classes. Whatever rules I have for one, I have for all. So, because not all bodies are created "equal", I have implemented a no belly and "derrière divide" rule. That is, all bellies, backs and hindquarters must be covered (even the good ones) at all times.

It really all boils down to this . . . students who are not dressed appropriately, which represents an outward physical expression of readiness, are probably not mentally or emotionally prepared, which is the more important inner personal state of readiness. That "readiness" is embodied in someone who has and shows respect for the basic concept of learning as well as the discipline they are engaged in. Yes, we're right back to that respect thing. Here's the thing . . .

THiNG # 33

THE WAY ONE DRESSES BOTH REFLECTS AND AFFECTS THE WAY ONE THiNKS, WHiCH iN TURN iNFLUENCES THE WAY ONE WORKS!

It's very simple; it all starts with a mindset, which in turn influences the way one prepares and approaches their work, which impacts the eventual outcome/result.

In an interview in Time Magazine, dated Aug. 2, 2010, the star of the hit T.V. show *Mad Men*, John Hamm, had this response to a question on how playing the part of Don Draper influenced his personal style: "I'm more conscious of what goes into dressing up. My personal style is not quite up to snuff with *Mad Men*. But the difference between a nice suit and a suit that isn't tailored to fit you is significant. It's very much a statement about a person who's ready to look like he's in control of a situation."

This last sentence is very important: "It's very much a statement about a person who's ready to look like he's in control of a situation". Remember that and we'll come back to the "look" factor later.

Many of our colleagues believe we take our "dress code" thing too far, that we're stifling our student's "creativity". I believe they don't take it far enough and, by not having any kind of dress standard, they are contributing to an atmosphere that produces a poor work ethic and fosters disrespect, which ultimately stifles progress. Especially in the beginning stages, but it applies to all levels of training, respect and discipline trump any individual's so-called "creativity". Learning to dance requires a long-term investment of many, many years. There is plenty of time for creativity in the dance-training program after one begins "mastering" the technique(s), but first things first.

The Rawles' dress code philosophy . . .

Before I go any further, let me reveal our philosophy on, for, and about the dress code. I boiled it down to a rather long (my preferred style) sentence: **"One should dress like a dancer, in order to look like a dancer, so one will feel like a dancer, and in turn act like a dancer, so one will train like a dancer, all toward the desired goal of becoming a dancer!"** (Dennonism #33) Simple, huh?

It is hard enough to become an accomplished dancer (or anything for that matter) without doing everything one can possibly do in order to become one, and that includes dressing the part. Most people already know that the way one dresses affects the way one acts in any given situation, and it's one's behavior that's most important when endeavoring to learn something.

As I mentioned previously, actors (even those trained in the "Method") appreciate the importance of what one wears when playing a given role. They know that what you wear can be the catalyst that puts you over the top in believing you are a given character. In other words, James Bond is James Bond because of the tuxedo and the martini (shaken, not stirred), not to mention the beautiful woman (or two or three) he tends to wear on each arm. The Hell's Angel motorcycle gang member needs a Harley, a leather jacket, jeans, and possibly a bandanna. It's easier to play a princess when you're dressed in a beautiful ball gown and have a tiara on your head. If you're going to play the part of a politician, you want to make sure you have both your faces securely fastened in order to be able to speak out of both sides of your mouth at the same time. No doubt about it, it really helps to become someone or something when you look like the someone or something you're trying to become.

As you may have guessed by now, it is my contention that the three main dance disciplines I continually speak of -- Ballet, Jazz, Modern -- should have a standardized set of requirements within each school/studio, which helps to cultivate a cohesive dance program. Among the requirements would be a specified "outfit" for each discipline and level. I'm going to break down the dress code that reputable schools usually have in place, as well as the ones that Sayhber and I impose on our classes. You may not agree with it and us, but you'll have a much better understanding of our reasoning. See what you think.

Let's talk Ballet first . . .

You'll find in a serious, reputable Ballet institution that each level has a particular color leotard each child must wear. They all wear pink tights. The boys usually wear a white "t" shirt with black tights no matter their level. The girls wear pink shoes and the boys wear black, sometimes white. The girls all have their hair tied securely in the traditional ballet bun.

This is how I explain it: **"The purpose of wearing leotards and tights in class is so you can be as naked as possible, without really being naked!"** (Dennonism #34)

That's it—to be "naked", with no part of the body hiding! It is extremely important that every muscle, bone and tendon be revealed in order for the instructor, and eventually the student, to see and determine whether a given part of the body is doing exactly what it's supposed to do at any given moment.

Of course the other, very important, reason to wear a leotard and tights is so you look like a ballet dancer. Yes, a student of the ballet should look like a ballet dancer, so he or she will feel like a ballet dancer, and in turn act like a ballet dancer, so he or she will train like a ballet dancer, all toward the desired goal of becoming a ballet dancer. Capiche?

Wearing the hair up in a bun (for the girls) has its practical as well as aesthetic reasons. First off, having the hair fastened securely up in a bun gives a look of elegance and beauty—the very essence of Ballet. It keeps the hair from getting in the dancer's face and eyes, which is important in order to know where one is in time and space, especially when doing the many kinds of turns one eventually does. It also helps make the dancer more aware of her own neck and spine thereby encouraging her to keep lifting and stand tall. Ballet students are constantly being reminded of their placement and posture and are continually asked to stretch their necks to gain the ever so important "swan like" appearance.

It needs to be understood that the technique that Ballet dancers work so hard to acquire requires a great amount of kinesiological understanding, so being stripped of all unnecessary, unrelated clothing and accessories, including jewelry, so as to make one as "naked" as possible is essential. The rule is simple: there should be nothing worn on the student that interferes, distracts or detracts from what the student is there to do, which is to learn to dance Ballet.

The wearing of specific colors for specific levels also has its purposes. One reason is to have an immediate identifying way to recognize which class/level a dancer belongs in. Everyone working at a given school would know to which class and teacher a student belongs by the color they're wearing. The second reason is akin to the different colored belts that are awarded in Martial Arts, the black belt being the ultimate prize. Being able to wear a particular colored leotard that has been designated for a higher level is the same as being awarded the next color up (level) belt in Martial Arts. The prize, if the school is reputable, is not given out easily. As everything else in life, it should be earned.

Now, let's talk about Modern dance . . .

As I've already explained, Modern was born out of a desire to not be Ballet. The early pioneers of Modern wanted to make creative, artistic dance works that were less fairytale-like (like many early ballets) and more real or "down to earth".

Fundamentally, Modern and Ballet take a completely different approach to expressing their art and discipline. Ballet is "turned out" and danced on the toes. Modern is parallel, with no turnout (generally) and danced with bare feet. Ballet has this "up" look and feel, where everything is lifted and perfectly balanced. Modern contracts, leans off balance, and uses a lot of floor work to express itself. Whereas Ballet, with its tutus and pointe shoes, endeavors to reflect the beauty in life (swans, princes, princesses and the like), Modern sets out to reflect the harsh, cold reality most "real" people experience.

Serious Modern dance programs will have their students dress only in leotards and tights that have the feet cut out—not in baggy shorts and baggy "t" shirts. That's their uniform. It's what Modern dancers wear. Like Ballet dancers, wearing only leotards and tights allows them to be naked (without really being naked) so their instructor can see every muscle, tendon and bone in order to determine if everything is working as it should.

The stripping away of all "normal" or "civilian" clothing and accoutrements serves to symbolize the stripping away of unnecessary frills we all tend to cover ourselves in, which basically serve to mask or camouflage our "real" or "inner" selves. The objective is to get down to, or find, our basic human core essence. That's what Modern dance endeavors to do: get to, and express on stage, the unfiltered, non-pasteurized reality of life . . . at least as they view it. Jewelry, unless purposely worn as a costume for a particular role, only serves to detract from that endeavor. As for color distinctions for levels, that's up to individual instructors.

Because Modern dance is a discipline that is usually taken up when entering college (where this form of dance essentially lives) or, at the earliest, when one enters their mid-to-late teens at a private studio, it's harder to develop a program analogous to Ballet. I personally do not recommend it for young ones under the age of 13. Modern dance often likes to "break the rules" of convention in its movement and expression. I'm an advocate of learning the rules first before breaking them, so therefore I recommend that young ones who are serious about their dancing stay in the fairy tale arena of Ballet until such techniques are forever embedded.

Now, let's talk about Jazz dance . . .

What sets Sayhber and me apart from most of our contemporaries these days is that we insist our students wear dancewear—no street clothes. The color scheme for our Jazz classes is black. Everything the student wears must be black. We have the ladies wear floor length, form-fitting, jazz pants, a leotard, and jazz shoes. The ladies may also wear a form-fitted "t" shirt over the leotard as long as it fits as tightly as the leotard itself. The men must wear black jazz pants or black sweats that fit like jazz pants with a black form-fitting "t" shirt. The dancers may wear a black sweatshirt on extremely cold days that will eventually be removed as their bodies warm.

Like Ballet and Modern instructors, we Jazz teachers need to see every inch of our students' bodies if we're going to be able to help them. Here it is again: I want them to dress like a Jazz dancer, so they'll look like a Jazz dancer, so they'll feel like a Jazz dancer, so they'll act like a Jazz dancer, while they train like a Jazz dancer, so they eventually become a Jazz dancer. Pretty insane, huh?

So why the color black? . . .

There are two main reasons we decided to go with all black for our Jazz classes. First off, we agree with Musical Theater icon Bob Fosse, who often had his dancers dress in black. He himself always wore black. He believed (as we do) it was slimming and showed the dancer's "line" off best. Dancers work extremely hard to develop a good sense of "line", so it's helpful to be wearing an outfit that accentuates that "line".

The second reason I like black for Jazz has to do with the inherent characteristics of the dance itself. By nature, Jazz is intense, dynamic and sensuous—even downright sexy. It's confrontational, meaning it often aims to intimidate. What it is not, by nature, is apprehensive, tentative or fearful. For me, at its very core, the attitude of a jazz dancer is one of predator, not prey. Think of the black panther as it stalks its potential dinner. With every step, the cat's focus, concentration and intensity deepens. Then there's a sudden explosion of power as it goes from zero to its top speed in just seconds. There's a beautiful example of what I mean in a 1962 film entitled *Walk On The Wild Side* that uses the dramatic image of a black panther walking and stalking during the film's initial credits. Ladies and gentlemen, that's jazz!

To morph or not to morph . . .

Here's the important concept that I want everyone to understand. Regardless of what type of dance one is about to engage in, the very physical act of dressing like a dancer is an important, meaningful ritual that helps him or her to not only physically prepare but also -- equally as important, maybe more -- to mentally, emotionally and psychologically prepare.

The physical act of dressing the part helps the dancer to set/focus his or her mind on what they're about to do. Yes, the physical affects the psychological. The dancer is essentially engaging in a metamorphic act of peeling away his or her personal, non-dancer persona and putting on a whole new artistic, dancer persona. Isn't that what football players, baseball players, basketball players, and players of all sports do before practice—put on a uniform that is specifically designed for their sport? Putting on their uniform helps them mentally prepare, which any professional can attest is essential. Those in the military wear a uniform for the very same reasons. It helps to focus the mind.

There's one other important reason for students to be dressed in essentially the same garb. It's an equalizer. One's social/economic status cannot be determined when everyone is dressed the same. No one looks better or worse, richer or poorer, or smarter or dumber than anyone else. Everybody at least starts on an equal "footing". Here it is again, only in short hand: Dress to Look to Feel to Act to Train to Become.

Let's not forget the respect angle. I want those training with us to respect the art form/discipline they are engaged in. I want them to respect everything they do. That respect is demonstrated through specific, purposeful actions, not the least of which is dressing the part. I do not want a student of mine to think for one moment that taking a dance class, any dance class, requires no particular effort, preparation, or mindset.

When explaining the dress code at the beginning of the semester, I ask my classes: "Unless you work for yourself and you become financially independent, where are you going to work where there is not some kind of dress code?" In the corporate world there are the "business suits" for both men and women that are essential if you want to be taken seriously. Most restaurants have a dress code which often has a color scheme connected to it as well. Banks have dress codes, as do most retail stores. Be thankful you're not working for Hot Dog on a Stick where you have to wear a beanie on your head with a hot dog attached. That's the real world out there (the world we teachers should be preparing our students for) . . . a world with a dress code.

Shuffling on to Tap . . .

There's not the need for as strict a dress code for Tap classes. The emphasis in Tap is not so much with placement, body alignment, and the aesthetic of "line", so it is not as important to be "naked". Yes, one always needs good placement and a good sense of "line", but it is in the Ballet, Jazz, and Modern classes where you would specifically work those techniques. The Tap class is primarily concerned with learning and developing a good sense of rhythm along with the clarity of execution of the many Tap steps.

Generally, what I have my students wear for Tap, aside from the obvious Tap shoes, are comfortable clothes they don't mind sweating in. Both the men and women are required to wear pants (jeans are fine) so they can move about freely, unencumbered. I do ask that no one's pants cover their shoes so I can see what their feet are doing at all times. In addition to hearing them tap, I need to see their feet, for how they use their feet is very important in the execution of a tap sound/step. "T" shirts, as long as they cover their tops and have no offensive writing on them, are perfectly acceptable.

The schizophrenic nature of Tap . . .

Although the distinctions are often blurred, Tap can be separated into three major categories. There's the traditional "Show Tap", then there's the "Rhythm" or "Jazz Tap", and then there's the more contemporary "Funk/Street Tap" style/method. Each is Tap, but each has it's own basic "flavor" or "feel" which brings about different methods and techniques to teaching and learning these styles. Because each is different, each style or method might call for its own particular wardrobe.

Show Tap is fun tap. It's a style of Tap associated with such historical musicals as *42nd Street*, which starred Ruby Keeler in the 1933 film, as well as such Broadway shows as Tommy Tune's 1983 production of *My One and Only*. This kind of tap is performed more on the toe taps, usually conveying or celebrating something fun. Fred Astaire and Gene Kelly (two of film's most famous star dancers) could be considered, in part, show tappers, as both were Broadway Musical/Revue performers before becoming famous in films. I say in part because they were both proficient in other dance forms, as well as being excellent singers and actors. They were also considerably more "theatrical" than most show tappers. Kelly integrated Ballet into much of his work, as well as daring feats (feets?) of athletics. Astaire utilized his amazing Ballroom partnering skills with a flare and finesse that is unmatched to this day and often crossed over, more than Kelly I believe, to a more Rhythm Tap style.

Rhythm or Jazz Tap utilizes the heeltap a lot more than "Show Tap" and has a heavier, more "into the ground", dynamic. Rhythm tappers are also very much Jazz musicians for they create rhythmic sound patterns with their taps that interplay with the music or, in some cases when dancing without accompaniment, they are the music. Basically, a Rhythm/Jazz Tapper is a percussionist. Early Tap pioneers, such as Honi Coles and Jimmy Slyde, as well as Sammy Davis Jr. and, a bit later, Gregory Hines -- well, the entire cast of the 1989 film *Tap* -- are supreme examples of this kind of Tap dance.

In a previous chapter I mentioned the magnificent Nicholas Brothers. They traversed back and forth between the theatrical Show Tap arena and the Rhythm Tap arena. Harold and Fayard Nicholas were extremely stylish, fantastically acrobatic, and beautifully artistic performers whose work still astounds to this day. As I said, they were extremely stylish, and that certainly manifested itself in the way they dressed.

Funk Tap came about as a natural result of the evolution of pop music. Savion Glover, who starred in the 1996 Broadway show, *Bring in 'Da Noise/Bring in' Da Funk*, was instrumental in the creation of this new style of tapping. Glover was a student and protégé of some of the great Rhythm Tappers, most notably, Gregory Hines. His desire was to bring Tap to a new level, making it relevant to a whole new generation. Australian group, Tap Dogs, is another example of this kind of dance. They both demonstrate how the art and discipline of Tap can be transformed and morphed into our present-day Hip-Hop culture.

Left: Dennon with partner Denise Cancino

Right: Sayhber with partner Rick McCullough

Let's pivot on over to Ballroom and Latin . . .

Because the way one dresses affects the way one feels and behaves, we advocate a pretty strict dress code for all our couples dance classes. We want our students to dress like they would if they were going to a "nice" upscale dance club. That would exclude jeans and "T" shirts, as well as sneakers and any kind of flip flop shoe. It's amazing how many strange looks I get when telling young men and women (high school and college age) that they need to dress up.

I'm about to say something I believe is critically important, but probably politically incorrect, so, one more time, you may want to close your eyes before you read this. What I tell the ladies is: "I want you dressed in such a way that would entice men to want to dance with you." I tell the men: "I want you dressed in such a way that when you approach, or are approached by, one of the ladies, their first reaction isn't, yuck-a-doodle!" Okay, you can open your eyes now.

Let's start with the ladies . . . The ladies must wear either a knee-length Ballroom skirt (nothing too short, too tight or too revealing) or nice pants (no jeans) with a non "T" shirt type top. We don't want the skirt too short for when the ladies do a quick turn, or a lay back dip, or if they should (yes it can and has happened) fall, they risk: **"Revealing a part of their 'inner personality' they'd probably wished they hadn't!" (Dennonism #35)**

Bellies and backs are to be covered at all times. In addition to the "some bellies ought never be seen" rule, this is so the men are not handling their bare backs when they partner up. The ladies must wear some kind of ballroom shoe or character heel, preferably no higher than two inches—definitely no spiked heels. The heels must have a secure ankle strap that'll hold the shoe securely to the foot.

There are a considerable number of ladies at the beginning of a semester, or at the beginning of a studio session, that cannot believe they have to wear heels. Obviously, many of these young ladies have never worn anything other than sneakers or flip-flops so they're leery of walking in them, let alone dancing in them. Well, as we tell them, it's about time they learn. We also inform them that ballroom/couples dancing is one of the last arenas to make a clear distinction between the masculine and feminine. If you've ever seen one of the amateur or professional competitions that are periodically shown on PBS, or the longtime hit *Dancing With The Stars*, you'll see how the obvious distinctions are "distinguished".

Now the men . . . The men must wear nice dress pants as well as a shirt with a collar. They need to have ballroom shoes or, if they already have them, they can use their jazz shoes. Again, they may not wear jeans, "T" shirts or sneakers. The ballroom shoes, as well as the jazz shoes, are dance shoes that have a special sole that is made for the dance floor. One is able to slide and glide along as necessary. Sneakers stick to the floor and inhibit one's ability to perform the footwork properly.

The Ballroom/Latin dress code all goes back to our original philosophy of having one **dress** like a Ballroom dancer, in order to **look** like a Ballroom dancer, in order to **feel** like a Ballroom dancer, so one will **act** like a Ballroom dancer, so one will **train** like a Ballroom dancer, all toward the desired goal of **becoming** a Ballroom dancer.

Hip-Hop . . .

When addressing my Ballet, Jazz, and Ballroom classes, I use Hip-Hop dancing as a perfect illustration of why one should dress the part. Since most teenagers and young adults are either "into" or, at minimum, aware of the Hip-Hop culture, they are also aware that a major part of what makes the Hip-Hop culture the Hip-Hop culture is the way one dresses. It actually begins with the music, which contributes to an attitude that manifests itself into a "look" which usually drives their parents and other adults insane—but I digress.

I ask my classes if they'd want to take a Hip-Hop class wearing Ballet tights or a tutu? How about a cowboy hat and boots? How about a Scottish kilt and a bagpipe? Of course not! Dressing the part helps one feel the part, which helps one assume the attitude, which helps one do the dance. We're right back where we began which is: to really learn Hip-Hop dancing, one must dress like a Hip-Hop dancer, so one looks like a Hip-Hop dancer, so one can feel like a Hip-Hop dancer, so one will act like a Hip-Hop dancer, so one will be motivated to train like a Hip-Hop dancer, all toward the goal of becoming a Hip-Hop dancer.

Conclusion . . .

It's up to us teachers to "educate" our students what it means to be respectful to the dance discipline they're studying, the school they're attending, their instructors, as well as all those who've played a role in the development of the dance discipline they're studying. We do this by what we have them do. The whole doing and showing respect thing ultimately leads to the "air of reverence" I continually speak of which fosters a much better atmosphere of learning—that which I call an "environment of excellence". Personally, I believe all subject matters would benefit from this kind of respect, but that's me and, apparently -- according to many -- I'm old-fashioned.

Though our dress code ideas may seem antiquated, I believe the case I've made for having one transcends time. Young ones (and not so young ones) need to be constantly taught, trained and reminded to be respectful, and what better way to start than by having them "dress the part". You may not believe it is conducive or practical for you to have as strict a dress code as I advocate for your classes (any workplace environment) but I do implore you to consider implementing some level of dress standards for your students to aspire to. Why not have your Ballet students dress like Ballet dancers, and your Jazz dancers dress like Jazz dancers, and your . . . well, you get the point.

Okay, you're almost finished. You're doing good, but, if you're up to it, there are some final, more personal, thoughts I'd like to leave you with.

IT'S A WRAP

FINAL THOUGHTS:
Are We Naked Yet?

REVERENCE:
With All Due Respect

INDEXES:
Things, Dennonisms, Steven's Sayings

CREDITS:
TV/Film/Theater/Concert/Published Works

Oil painting of Sayhber performing
Artist: Wally Bambrick

FINAL THOUGHTS
ARE WE NAKED YET?

I remember when Sayhber and I went in to meet actor Warren Beatty and director Barry Levinson. They were preparing a film about the notorious 1930s and 40s gangster Bugsy Siegel, appropriately entitled *Bugsy*. They needed a choreographer that understood the dances of that era and, with our background in film as well as our expertise in Latin and Ballroom dancing, we thought we stood as good a chance as anyone in getting the job.

Starting with the basic knowledge that Beatty was looking to learn the Tango, we began speculating what we might do to impress him. We did our best to get into his head. It's known that he was a trained "Method" actor, having studied with famed Stella Adler, and his reputation for being a "ladies man" was not exactly a highly guarded secret. He was also known to have been somewhat of an intellectual. In other words, he could hold his own in a discussion on most subjects. We knew if we were going to be selected from the many choreographers vying for the job, we had to be able to hold our own in a conversation about the period in question, as well as the dance itself. We also knew we had to present something that would appeal to both of his "special" interests—acting and women.

As was our usual practice when presented with an opportunity like this, we fully committed ourselves to doing our very best, which meant putting in the time and effort necessary to choreograph a dance that would represent our "expertise" on the subject. We ended up creating a dance that was both overtly dramatic and unabashedly sexy. Upon meeting Beatty and Levinson we put forth our best "intelligent" personas. After exchanging pleasantries, it was time to get down to business. We handed over our music and told them we had prepared a little something we hoped they'd like.

We then moved out onto the floor, gave the nod for the music to begin, focused in on each other and commenced to fill the room with all the intensity, emotion, and dynamics we could. We had already resolved, that whether what we did would appeal to them, we weren't going to hold anything back. No matter how much you prepare, you never really know what a director is looking for when you audition. All you can do is put yourself out there and go for it. That's what we did. We did a couple of lifts (a specialty of ours), a few throws, some fancy footwork, several dramatic dips, and concluded with a spectacular tornado-like pivot spin whereupon I finished by sliding Sayhber across the floor. Then, just to top it off, I dropped down on top of her to conclude the dance with a passionate kiss. Now if this didn't appeal to the famous Mr. Ladies Man, then nothing would.

There was a moment of silence as we held our final pose, then we got up and awaited a response. Warren did something that, when a star of his magnitude does, you know you've peaked his interest. He got up off his chair and began asking questions on how we did this certain move. I knew we had him where we wanted him because we weren't immediately dismissed (as normally happens) for them to confer about us. He liked this one particular position we did. It's a position where both partners are facing the same direction. It's a kind of Tango "spooning" where the two become one. By the way, we got this move from our hyper-macho mentor, for whom it was a kind of signature position. Thank you Steven Peck.

After we showed him a few things, we concluded the interview and went on our way. It wasn't long before we were notified to begin working with Warren. We spent many hours at his house teaching him how to Tango. He seemed to like the lessons—the sexier the moves, the better. One thing for sure, Sayhber spent a lot of time in his arms. It was an interesting experience, to say the least. I could tell you some intriguing stories about our time at his house, being with him, and the people we saw there, but he's married now to his co-star in the film, Annette Bening, and they have children, so as the saying goes, discretion is the better part of valor.

You want to know what the upshot of the whole experience was? When we got into the actual production of the film, they, he, somebody decided to change things and took out the Tango. I never did find out why. It could be that once filming began Warren was so busy with all the scenes he was involved in that he didn't have the time necessary to properly prepare the dance. It could have been that the film needed to be shortened, I don't know, but these kinds of things happen all the time. Warren ended up doing a much easier Fox Trot/Two Step instead.

Aside from teaching Beatty how to dance, our job was to work with his co-stars Annette Bening and Bebe Neuwirth so they'd look authentic to the period when they danced in the nightclub scenes. Both were and are elegant, gracious, extremely talented and a real pleasure to work with. We also had to prepare the background dancers who completed the nightclub scenes. It's too bad we couldn't finish what we started because, like most great actors, Beatty was an intense, excellent student and I'm sure it would have ended up being a wonderful cinematic Tango . . . oh well.

I've recounted this story not just to drop a few names. What I really wanted to do was illustrate how we put into practice what I call the "Ten Keys To Excellence" to contend for a highly coveted job. Whether we got the job or not, it was important we put forth our very best effort, an excellent effort, so that we could look ourselves in the mirror and respect the persons looking back. It worked out for us that time, but believe me, it doesn't always.

As I said in the Preface, this book was born principally out of frustration because of the inordinate amount of time we've had to spend in our classes teaching the basic principles of learning to those who, because of the number of years they've already spent in one or several learning institutions, should've known better. It's difficult to teach somebody how to do something if they've yet to learn what their part is in the teaching/learning process.

I've done my best to put down in writing our thoughts, theories and philosophies concerning the process of teaching and learning, and I do hope they'll be found useful. Ultimately, it's not important that you agree with me on everything. What I do hope is that I've inspired you to think deeper and clearer on how you can better your efforts to become the very best you possibly can be.

I must say, we've been heartened over the years to have had so many students express their gratitude for our "different" way of teaching. We've been told over and over again that because our lessons extend beyond the art and craft of dance -- you know, lessons that transcend the subject matter -- our students' work in all other areas has improved. This includes the academic class, the workplace, and even in one's personal life. It's all because they've gained a much better understanding of how they can, and must, take responsibility for their learning/achievements.

As I mentioned before, there isn't an "Excellence 101" class to be found anywhere. It's my desire for this book to help fill that void. I'm about to wrap things up here, but if you'll indulge me, I have one more very personal story for you.

Why this book almost didn't get completed . . .

When I began dabbling with the idea of writing a book, one of the things that motivated me was thinking how wonderful it would be to leave something like this to our darling daughter, Jessica. I thought that, long after Sayhber and I were gone, she'd have this book that contained our thoughts, theories and philosophies on art, dance, and the process connected with teaching and learning, as well as a few stories from our careers to remember us by. I knew that even if no one else would want it or appreciate it, she would . . . and that'd be good enough for me.

Our Jess had been dancing pretty much her entire life and became quite a wonderful performer. She had been watching us perform, choreograph, and teach since her birth, so I guess you could say it was in her blood. She heard us pontificate on matters of the arts, dance, and education her entire life. I just knew she was sure to understand my writings and hopefully even be encouraged by it. Jessica loved dancing and performing, but, unlike most of her peers, what she really enjoyed was teaching. She had the most contagious smile that would brighten up any room. She also had the most beautifully expressive arms, along with legs that went forever, and feet—sheer perfection! It became evident in her early adult life that she had a special God-given gift -- a calling, if you will -- to work with children. She taught all ages, all levels, but the young ones really loved her.

She was trained primarily by Louise Mandel who was director of the Pacific Dance Academy. Louise was a mentor to her, along with Tamara Gray, who headed up the lower-division children's department at the Performing Arts Center in Van Nuys, CA. Both these beautiful women took Jessica under their wings and helped her become an exceptional teacher, dare I say "educator". She acquired another mentor, Dr. Paula Thomson, at Cal State University of Northridge, CA, where she was majoring in Kinesiology.

As you may have figured out by my continual use of the past tense, we lost Jessica on August 8, 2008 due to a rare condition known as Marfan syndrome. She was twenty-seven years old. It was unexpected and completely devastating. We're not over it, and we never will be. Her mother and I will never be the same—never, ever. Because of this catastrophic event, I was numbed and stopped writing for over a year. I didn't know if I could ever begin again. Her mother and I had lost all desire in doing anything, except what was absolutely necessary in order to survive.

Please understand, as sad as we both are, we fully expect to see our beautiful Jessica one day in Heaven. I know she's still dancing, because her gifts are from God, and where better to express her beautiful talents, than in a place where her gifts originated.

After a year or so went by, I began wondering if I should open up the book file and dust it off. Who would I leave the book to? Did I have the desire, let alone the energy, to complete a project that I knew would take more out of me than dance ever did?

As Sayhber and I continued our teaching at various places, we often found ourselves letting off steam by sharing stories on how much time and effort we had to put into teaching our students how to be effective learners. Day after day, week after week, more than ever, we found ourselves teaching on matters of respect, responsibility, accountability—well, pretty much everything we've discussed in this book.

On occasion I'd catch myself assuring someone that I was writing a book that would contain all the principles we teach, but the book wasn't really progressing. There definitely seemed to be a need for a resource like this one, but still, did I have it in me?

After considerable prayer, it came to me that my daughter would want me to finish what I started. After all, that is what her mother and I have always tried to teach her and her brother—to finish what you start. So, for her, I began in earnest again to finish this project. Whenever faced with a situation like this, I always think back to one of the most important lessons I learned from our Steven Peck. Completing a job one has begun is in and of itself: **"An exercise in character development!" (Steven's saying #10)**

You see, I had to finish this book in order to show myself that I am capable and strong. When the time comes, I want to be able to look my beautiful Jess in the eye (after I've given her the biggest, longest hug possible) and tell her I finished what I started and that, for better or worse, I completed the project I set out to do.

Well, there you have it—a bit of history on my journey in writing this book. I put forth our thoughts, theories and philosophies, and argued their validity as best I could. It's for you to decide if what I've written has merit.

Final conclusion . . .

You should know that I'm not a college graduate. I've been hired to teach at various universities and colleges based on my professional experience. Because a dancer's career is relatively short, we have to take the work when it comes, and that's what we did. Please understand, Broadway, Films, and Television cares very little about a college degree. It's only your talent, hard work, and perseverance that concern these. As a young person I started working a lot, and the on-the-job education and training I received from working with the very best that Stage, Film, and Television had to offer has garnered me an education you cannot get at any school.

Don't get me wrong . . . I am an advocate of higher education. We're extremely proud that our daughter continued her education, and earned enough credits before she left us to receive her Bachelor of Science degree in kinesiology from CSUN. It's just that our lives took a different course and, because of that, we are able to pass down real nuggets of gold that can only be obtained from "real world", having been in the trenches, experience.

To the extent it's possible, I've endeavored to write as close to how I speak as possible. The only difference is, when I speak, the words usually aren't spelled correctly. Anyway, I hope what I've written is considered helpful. Ultimately, what matters most to me is that I put myself out there; first *on the floor*, where I put in the time to do the work, and now *on the line*, for everyone to judge.

Okay, I'm done -- you're done -- stick a fork in us, we are totally finished. We're losing light so I gotta wrap things up, but I have just one more question for you: **Are we naked yet?** By now you ought to have a pretty good idea of what makes us tick. I've pretty much exposed our inner-most thoughts. Love us, or hate us, this is who we are and will continue to be till we dance ourselves onto that great dance floor in the sky.

Say goodnight Gracie . . .

Let me sign off by recounting the words of my favorite funny man, the great Red Skelton, whom I was so fortunate to meet and dance for when he was inducted into the Comedy Hall of Fame. At the conclusion of each of his weekly television shows, he would show his gratitude and respect for his audience by saying: "Goodnight and may God Bless! Goodnight."

Dennon with The Steven Peck Jazz Company, Coronet Theater Los Angeles
late 1970s - Photo: Unknown

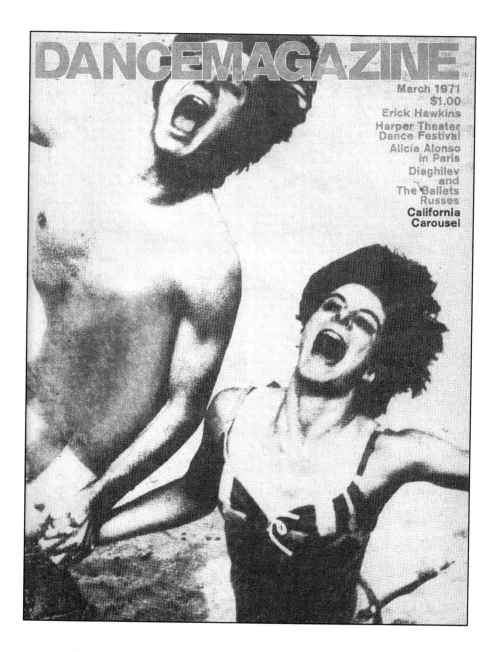

19-year-old Sayhber with Tony Curreri on cover of Dance Magazine
Rehearsing a scene from an original musical entitled:
Above the Garbage for Steven Peck Dance Company
Photo: Robert Lurie

REVERENCE
WiTH ALL DUE RESPECT

We'd like to pay our respects to the many talented choreographers and directors we've had the privilege to work for. These men and women were our "professors" in the classroom of stage, film, and television. Some names we'd like to acknowledge are: Toni Basil, Joe Bennett, Mel Brooks, Tony Charmoli, Don Crichton, Ron Field, Rob Iscove, Alan Johnson, Michael Kidd, Hugh Lambert, Barry Levinson, Walter Painter, Charlene Painter, Ron Poindexter, Jaime Rogers, Scott Salmon, Robert Sidney, Sylvester Stallone, Tony Stevens, Bob Thompson, and of course our mentor, creative father, and most loving friend, Mr. Steven Peck.

We don't want to forget the hundreds of professional dancers (our peers) that we've worked with over the years. They are too numerous to mention by name, but please know, we are extremely appreciative.

We've been blessed with many excellent teachers over the years. Thank you: Aggie Auld, the folks at Call's Fine Arts Center, Bobby Banas, Joe Bennett, Skippy Blair, Patrick Frantz, Hama, Margaret Graham Hills, Stanley Holden, Charles Moore, Patricia Standard, the original members of the Steven Peck Jazz Company, Jaime Rogers, Buddy Schwimmer, Audrey Share, Suzanne Skeel, Joe Tremaine, and so many, many more.

We also want to acknowledge the enthusiastic and supportive dancers who became part of our original dance revue, "Energy Force", and our subsequent concert company, Jazz Dancers, Inc., for the sixteen years we operated. Let me extend a special thank you to two very special people, Nela Fry and Erica Jordan—for without their enthusiasm, expertise, and dedication, we couldn't have operated.

We must also acknowledge our long-time dance assistant Debbie Munz. Thank you for your constant support, your high energy, and amazing dependability. To Ryan Garcia, our website designer/webmaster, you have our eternal gratitude. Thank you for being there for us.

Finally, I'd like to thank *those precious, exceptional, excellent few* who helped us put this book together. Thank you: Ashley Rae Bergin for your love, artistry and the many hours you put into this project. Matt Rawles for your creative, funny illustrations. You make me proud. Bethany Tidwell for your artistry and technical skill in completing the artwork process. Stacy Taylor for your editing time, expertise, and constant support. And of course, our Jessica, who always made me feel I could do it.

To all those names we've mentioned as well as the many names space doesn't allow, Sayhber and I would like to curtsy and bow respectively. I hope you can hear our applause, because it's loud. With appreciation and deepest respect.

Dennon and Sayhber Rawles

Jazz Dancers, Inc. Publicity Photo: Paul Da Silva
Dennon & Sayhber

BIOGRAPHY

Dennon and Sayhber Rawles have gained international recognition for their work as choreographers, performers, and dance instructors, with credits in Japan, Brazil, Argentina, Canada, and Hollywood. They have choreographed five feature films including John Travolta's *Staying Alive* and *Bugsy*, starring Warren Beatty. They choreographed for Ann-Margret's Las Vegas Show in which Dennon was a featured performer. They've also choreographed for Television Sit-Coms and have several commercials to their credit.

As performers they have worked with some of the biggest stars on Broadway and in Hollywood, including: Carol Burnett, Cyd Charisse, Janet Jackson, Cheryl Ladd, Liza Minnelli, Ann-Margret, Rita Moreno, the Nicholas Brothers, Bernadette Peters, Juliette Prowse, Tommy Tune, Dick Van Dyke, and Raquel Welch. Dennon was a featured performer on both Baryshnikov T.V. specials in the 1980s and has appeared in such films as Mel Brooks' *History of the World, Part One*, Martin Scorsese's *New York, New York*, and *The Best Little Whorehouse in Texas*, which starred Burt Reynolds and Dolly Parton. Among the over 100 Television shows they've appeared in separately or together are: The Academy Awards Show (four times), American Music Awards, People's Choice Awards, two Dick Clark Specials, two Dean Martin Christmas Specials, The Barbara Mandrell Series, and The Carol Burnett Show.

They've choreographed several stage musicals including: *Bells Are Ringing, Carnival, Damn Yankees, Guys and Dolls, Into The Woods, South Pacific*, and *West Side Story*. From the mid 1990s through the mid 2000s they wrote, directed and choreographed original Musical Revues for Moorpark Community College. Over the years they've also been commissioned to create many concert works for Universities, Colleges and Dance Companies.

Company directors . . .

The Rawles' established their first company, Energy Force, in 1977. Noted for it's high energy, the group performed at dance clubs throughout L.A. and Orange County. In 1979 they formed, what was at the time, the only professional Jazz Dance Concert Company in Southern California, Jazz Dancers, Inc. (JDI). For 13 years they created and performed numerous original jazz works at Universities, Colleges and Auditoriums, touring locally as well as guest performing at the World Jazz Dance Congress, in Evanston, Ill.

Teaching . . .

The Rawles' have been teaching (separately and sometimes together) since the early 1970s. They have at one time or other been on staff at many studios throughout Orange, L.A., and Ventura Counties, including: Steven Peck Studios in L.A. and Fullerton, Dupree Dance Academy in W.L.A., and Studio F in Burbank, CA, Agoura Hills Dance Center, and Westside Ballet in Santa Monica, Performing Arts Center in Van Nuys, Dance Dimensions in Woodland Hills, and Inspire Dance Studio in Simi Valley.

Some of the colleges and universities they've taught at include: UCLA, USC, Cal State Long Beach, Loyola Marymount University, Moorpark College, Orange Coast College, Long Beach Community College, Pierce College, Alan Hancock College, and Cerritos College.

THiNG INDEX

DENNONISMS

EVEN MORE DENNONiSMS

The following did not make it into the book. They are usually directed to my "favortie" students.

\#1   "I'D PAY 50 CENTS TO SEE THAT . . . AFTER YOU PAID ME $20 TO COME WATCH!"

\#2   "A RELAXED BODY MEANS A RELAXED BRAIN—GET OFF THE BARRE!"

\#3   "WHERE DID YOUR MOTHERS AND I GO WRONG?"

\#4   "ONE LAST TIME BEFORE WE DO IT AGAIN!"

\#5   "THE SLOWER WE GO . . . THE LONGER IT TAKES!"

\#6   "JUST WHO DO I THINK YOU ARE?"

\#7   "I SAID IT TWO WEEKS AGO, I SAID IT LAST WEEK AND . . . I SAID IT NEXT WEEK!"

\#8   "PRACTICE! IT'S NOT LIKE YOU'RE ANY GOOD!"

\#9   "YOU'RE MY FAVORITE . . . I DON'T CARE A WIT ABOUT THE OTHERS!"

\#10   "IF YOU CAN'T DO IT . . . IT'S PROBABLY BECAUSE YOU DON'T HAVE THE ABILITY!"

STEVEN'S SAYiNGS

By the way, there are other, more "intriguing" sayings, but I wanted to keep the book PG!

TV/FILM/THEATER/CONCERT/PUBLISHED WORKS

TELEVISION & VIDEO

YEAR	TITLE	CHOREOGRAPHER
1974	*TELEVISION SPECIAL* (Title unknown) – CBS T.V. (Sayhber)	Jaime Rogers
	46th ANNUAL ACADEMY AWARDS SHOW (Dennon w/Liza Minnelli & Connie Stevens)	Ron Field
1976	*DEAN MARTIN CHRISTMAS SPECIAL* – NBC T.V. (Dennon)	Robert Sydney
	NOONTIME SHOW – KCBS T.V. L.A. (D & S promoting an upcoming Tito Puente tribute)	Steven Peck
	DICK CLARK'S BANDSTAND SPECIAL – ABC T.V. (Dennon w/artists from 50s & 60s)	Ron Poindexter
	MERV GRIFFIN SHOW – Syndication Taped at Caesars Palace, L.V. (Dennon w/Rita Moreno)	Ron Poindexter
1977	*ANN-MARGRET'S RHINESTONE COWBOY SPECIAL* (Dennon featured partnering Ann-Margret)	Rob Iscove
	AMERICAN CRITICS AWARDS - Syndication (Dennon with Ben Vereen)	Ron Field
	VICTOR AWARDS - Syndication Professional Sports Awards (Ann-Margret Dancers performed)	Not known
	CBS FALL PREVIEW SPECIAL (Dennon & Sayhber with Dick Van Dyke)	Joe Bennett
	DICK CLARK T.V. SPECIAL – ABC T.V. (Dennon w/artists from 50s & 60s)	Ron Poindexter
	THE CARPENTERS AT CHRISTMAS – ABC T.V. (Dennon)	Bob Thompson
	DEAN MARTIN'S CHRISTMAS IN CALIFORNIA - NBC T.V. (Dennon)	Hugh Lambert
	CBSs 50th ANNIVERSARY SPECIAL (Dennon)	Alan Johnson
	ABCs SILVER ANNIVERSARY SPECIAL (Dennon and Sayhber featured)	Ron Poindexter
1978	*SUPER NIGHT AT THE SUPERBOWL* – CBS T. V. (Dennon w/Joe Namath, Paul Williams)	Walter Painter
	5th ANNUAL AMERICAN MUSIC AWARDS – ABC T.V. (Sayhber assists choreographer & is featured)	Ron Poindexter
	35th GOLDEN GLOBE AWARDS - Beverly Hilton Hotel (Dennon & Sayhber)	Ron Poindexter
	STEVE AND EYDIE CELEBRATE IRVINE BERLIN Steve Lawrence & Eydie Gorme – NBC T.V. (Dennon featured w/ballerina Leslie Browne)	Rob Iscove
	100 YEARS OF RECORDED MUSIC – NBC T.V. (Dennon & Sayhber – Dennon featured w/Sandy Duncan)	Rob Iscove
	30th DIRECTORS GUILD AWARD SHOW (Dennon w/Ann-Margret)	Unknown
	$100,000 NAME THAT TUNE (39 half-hour shows – Dennon featured)	Dennon Rawles
	DICK CLARK LIVE T.V. SPECIAL - ABC T.V. (Sayhber assists choreographer and is featured)	Ron Poindexter

1979	6th ANNUAL AMERICAN MUSIC AWARDS – ABC T.V. (Sayhber assists choreographer and is featured)	Ron Poindexter
	THE JEFFERSON'S – CBS T.V. "Every Night Fever" (Dennon & Sayhber)	Ron Poindexter
	CHERYL LADD SPECIAL – ABC T.V. (Dennon w/Cheryl Ladd & Ben Vereen)	Ron Field
	PRESENTING SUSAN ANTON – CBS T.V. (4 Show Spring Variety Series – Dennon)	Walter Painter
	CAROL BURNETT AND COMPANY – CBS T. V. (4 Show Summer Variety Series – Dennon)	Don Crichton
	COUNTRY CHRISTMAS SPECIAL (Location shoot in Tulsa, OK – Dennon featured)	Don Crichton
	PLAYBOY MANSION T.V. SPECIAL (Dennon & Sayhber Performed at the Mansion)	Dennon & Sayhber
	PERRY COMO'S CHRISTMAS IN NEW MEXCIO – ABC T.V. (Location shoot in Albuquerque, N.M. – Dennon featured)	Don Crichton
	BOONE FAMILY CHRISTMAS SPECIAL - ABC T.V. (Sayhber assists choreographer)	Maria Gava
1980	BARYSHNIKOV ON BROADWAY – ABC T.V. (Dennon featured w/Baryshnikov, Liza Minnelli)	Ron Field
	7th ANNUAL AMERICAN MUSIC AWARDS – ABC T.V. (Sayhber assists choreographer and performs)	Ron Poindexter
	BECAUSE WE CARE T.V. SPECIAL - CBS T.V. (Show to help Cambodia – Dennon)	Rob Iscove
	THE BIG SHOW – NBC 90 minute Variety Series (4 one hr. Shows – Dennon)	Rob Iscove
	CHEERLEADING T.V. SPECIAL – ABC T.V. (Dennon and Sayhber)	Scott Salmon
	ME AND MAX – NBC T.V. Series (Sayhber works as stand-in)	no choreographer
	NBCs PEACOCK SPECIAL (Sayhber)	Ron Poindexter
	FROM RAQUEL WITH LOVE – ABC T.V. (Raquel Welch T.V. Special – Dennon)	Tony Charmoli
	BARE TOUCH OF MAGIC – Canadian T.V. (Dennon and Sayhber featured performers)	Rob Iscove
1981	BARBARA MANDRELL AND THE MANDRELL SISTERS (2 one hour shows - Dennon) – NBC T.V.	Scott Salmon
	7th ANNUAL PEOPLE'S CHOICE AWARDS – NBC T.V. (Dennon and Sayhber)	Unknown
	53rd ANNUAL ACADEMY AWARDS SHOW – ABC T.V. (Dennon w/Lucy Arnaz & Irene Cara)	Walter Painter
	CBS AFFILIATES SHOW – CBS T.V. (Dennon – Special to promote new shows)	Don Crighton
	BARYSHNIKOV IN HOLLYWOOD - CBS T.V. (Dennon w/Baryhsnikov, Bernadette Peters, Gene Wilder)	Michael Kidd
	BARBARA MANDRELL AND THE MANDRELL SISTERS (2 one hour shows - Dennon) – NBC T.V.	Scott Salmon
	MAGIC WITH THE STARS - NBC T.V. (Dennon w/David Copperfield)	Don Crichton
1982	BARBARA MANDRELL AND THE MANDRELL SISTERS (2 one hour shows - Dennon) - NBC T.V.	Scott Salmon
	39th GOLDEN GLOBE AWARDS SPECIAL (Taped at Beverly Hilton Hotel – Dennon)	Don Crichton
	54th ANNUAL ACADEMY AWARDS SHOW (Dennon w/Gregory Hines & Debbie Allen)	Alan Johnson

	ANN JILLIAN VARIETY SHOW – PILOT	Kevin Carlisl
	(Dennon)	
	TEXACO STAR THEATER VARIETY SHOW – NBC T.V.	Alan Johnson
	(Dennon)	
	PONTIAC INDUSTRIAL SHOW	Alan Johnson
	(Dennon w/Dick Van Dyke, Ann Jillian)	
1984	*BRAHMA BEER COMMERCIAL*	The Rawles'
	(Filmed in Rio De Janeiro for Brazilian T.V.)	
	STAR SEARCH – CBS T.V.	no choreographer
	(Dennon was a judge)	
1985	*DIET SLICE COMMERCIAL*	Dennon Rawles
	(National commercial)	
	ALFRED HITCHCOCK PRESENTS - NBC T.V.	Unknown
	(Linda Pearl – Dennon plays her dance teacher)	
	SHOWA SHELL COMMERCIAL	The Rawles'
	(Filmed in Tokyo for Japanese T.V.)	
1986	*A LOOK BACK* - NBC T.V. Special	Scott Salmon
	(Dennon & Sayhber)	
1988	*60th ANNUAL ACADEMY AWARDS SHOW* – ABC T.V.	Michael Kidd
	(Dennon w/Little Richard, Bill Medley, Jennifer Warnes)	
	SMOTHERS BROTHERS REUNION SPECIAL – CBS T.V.	Ron Poindexter
	(Dennon)	
	ANHEUSER-BUSCH INDUSTRIAL	Scott Salmon
	(Dennon)	
1989	*COMEDY HALL OF FAME T.V. SPECIAL*	Scott Salmon
	(Tribute to Red Skelton, w/Tommy Tune – Dennon)	
1990	*ALRIGHT* - Janet Jackson Music Video	Michael Kidd
	(Dennon assists choreographer and performs	
	w/Cab Calloway, Cyd Charisse, Nicholas Bros.)	
1994	*SHOWTIME COMMERCIAL*	Dennon Rawles
	(Dennon featured promoting Cable Network)	
1996	*TEMPORARILY YOURS* – CBS T.V.	Sayhber Rawles
	Starred Debi Mazar (choreo'd comedy cha-cha)	
	MR. RHODES – NBC T.V.	Sayhber Rawles
	(Choreo'd Salsa dance w/Ron Glass & Farrah Forke)	
	HANGTIME - NBC T.V.	The Rawles'
	(choreographed spoof of Saturday Night Fever)	
	GOOSEBUMPS: ESCAPE FOM HORRORLAND	Dennon Rawles
	(Video Game featuring Jeff Goldblum)	
1999	*THE TIME OF YOUR LIFE* - FOX T.V. Drama Series	Smith Wordes
	(Starred Jennifer Love-Hewitt – Dennon & Jessica)	

FILM

1976	*NEW YORK, NEW YORK* – United Artists	Ron Field
	(Starring Liza Minnelli, Robert DeNiro	
	directed by Martin Scorsese – Dennon)	

1980	*HISTORY OF THE WORLD, PART I* – 20th Century Fox (Directed by and starring Mel Brooks – Dennon)	Alan Johnson
1982	*BEST LITTLE WHOREHOUSE IN TEXAS* – Universal Pictures (Starring Dolly Parton, Burt Reynolds, directed by: Colin Higgins – Dennon)	Tony Stevens
1982 – 83	*STAYING ALIVE* – Paramount Pictures (Starring John Travolta, directed by: Sylvester Stallone – Dennon and Sayhber)	The Rawles'
1983	*VOYAGE OF THE ROCK ALIENS* (Starring Pia Zadora and Craig Sheffer) directed by: James Fargo	The Rawles'
1984	*JAILBIRD* aka *PRISON DANCER* (Filmed in Buenos Aires, Argentina) *KING OF THE CITY* aka *CLUB LIFE* (Starring Tony Curtis & Dee Wallace)	The Rawles' The Rawles'
1991	*BUGSY* - TriStar Pictures (Starring Warren Beatty, Annette Bening, directed by: Barry Levinson)	The Rawles'
1995	*DRACULA: DEAD AND LOVING IT* – Columbia Pictures (Starring Leslie Nielsen, directed by Mel Brooks)	Alan Johnson

THEATER, NiGHT CLUB, & STAGE REVUES

1974	*THE TONY MARTIN AND CYD CHARISE SHOW* (Dennon – National tour including Thunderbird Hotel, L.V.)	Ron Field
1976	*TRIBUTE TO TITO PUENTE* – At My Place, Beverly Hills D & S w/Steven Peck Dance Co. w/Tito Puente Band	Steven Peck
1977	*BELLS ARE RINGING* (Pacific Palisades High School) TONI BASIL SHOW – Sahara Hotel, L.V. (Dennon & Sayhber)	The Rawles' Toni Basil The Rawles'
1977 – 79	*ENERGY FORCE* - Dance revue (5 -7 member co. performing in Discos throughout L.A., Orange, and Ventura Counties)	The Rawles'
1978	*YOU REMIND ME OF A FRIEND* (Original musical choreographed by Sayhber) *GYPSY* (Pierce College – outdoor production)	Sayhber Rawles Sayhber Rawles
1979 - 81	*THE ANN-MARGRET SHOW* – National Tour (Dennon - 3 years as featured performer)	Rob Iscove Walter Painte
1981	*THE ANN-MARGRET SHOW* – Ceasar's Palace, L.V. (Choreographed a 9 minute Latin production number in which Dennon was featured with Ann-Margret)	The Rawles'

1981	FRENCH FASHION SHOW REVUE (Held at Chez Moi club in Beverly Hills)	The Rawles'
1987	DENNON & SAYHBER AND CO (40 min. Revue produced & directed by the Rawles') 6 Tuesday night performances at world famous Chippendales)	The Rawles'
1990	NOKODA U.S.A. TRADE SHOW (Rawles' peform Tango and Salsa)	The Rawles'
1991	THE ORGANIZED MALE – an original Musical Coast Playhouse, Ho., Ca	Dennon Rawles
1992	JAZZED UP – Dance revue for Japan featuring the music of Rob Mullins - Ann Germaine: producer)	The Rawles'
1995	CHARLIE C – an original musical by Steven Peck (Vanguard Theater, Fullerton, CA)	The Rawles'
1997	FASHION SHOW at CHEZ MOI, Beverly Hills, CA (choreographed 2 dance numbers)	The Rawles
1999	SWEET CHARITY – Moorpark College (Staged & choreographed)	Sayhber Rawles
	ALL THAT'S JAZZ – an original revue (Staged and choreographed)	The Rawles'
2000	GUYS & DOLLS – Moorpark College (Staged & choreographed)	The Rawles'
	MAGIC TO DO – Moorpark College (Original Revue - directed & choreographed)	The Rawles'
	INTO THE WOODS – Moorpark College (Staged and choreographed)	Sayhber Rawles
2001	SOUTH PACIFIC – Moorpark College (Staged & choreographed)	The Rawles'
	PURE IMAGINATION – Moorpark College (Original Revue - directed & choreographed)	The Rawles'
	CARNIVAL – Moorpark College (Staged & choreographed)	The Rawles'
2002	WEST SIDE STORY – Moorpark College (Staged & choreographed)	The Rawles'
	BROADWAY DREAMS - Moorpark College (Original Revue - written, produced, directed)	The Rawles'
2003	FUNDRAISING FOLLIES '03 – Moorpark College (Original Revue - produced, directed, and staged)	The Rawles'
	WILD ON BROADWAY – Moorpark College (Original Revue – written, produced, directed)	The Rawles'
2005	BROADWAY RHYTHMS – Moorpark College (Original Revue - written, produced, directed)	The Rawles'
	DAMN YANKEES – Moorpark College (Staged & choreographed)	The Rawles'
2006	FUNDRAISING FOLLIES '06 – Moorpark College (Original Revue - produced, directed, and staged)	The Rawles'
	BEATLES ON BROADWAY – Moorpark College (Original Revue - written, produced, directed)	The Rawles'

2007	FUNDRAISING FOLLIES '07 – Moorpark College (Original Revue - produced, directed, and staged) MOON OVER BROADWAY – Moorpark College (Original Revue - written, produced, directed)	The Rawles' The Rawles'
2008	FUNDRAISING FOLLIES '08 – Moorpark College (Original Revue - produced, directed, and staged) FEARLESS ON BROADWAY – Moorpark College (Original Revue - produced, directed, and staged)	The Rawles' The Rawles'

CONCERT

1970 – 76	STEVEN PECK JAZZ COMPANY – a concert dance co. Sayhber was assistant choreographer & principal dancer. Dennon joined company in 1972. (Company performed original works to such artists as: George Gershwin, Tito Puente, & Gustav Holst)	Steven Peck
1979 – 92	JAZZ DANCERS, INC. (JDI) - a concert dance co. Directors & principal choreographers: Dennon & Sayhber Rawles (Choreographed 39 original works to such artists as: Dave Brubeck, Don Ellis, Pat Metheny, Stan Getz, Tito Puente, & Paul Simon)	The Rawles'

JDI was awarded several grants to create original works from: The California Arts Council, the L.A. Cultural Affairs Department, and the National/State/County Partnership. Various venues for performances include: USC Bovard Auditorium, UCLA Royce Hall, CSUN, Cerritos College, La Mirada Civic Auditorium, Barnsdall Park in Hollywood, CA, The Wilshire Ebell Theater, The Japan America Theater, Alan Hancock College, Plummer Auditorium in Fullerton, CA, and the World Jazz Dance Congress held in Evanston, Ill.

Sample Reviews:

"Upbeat and uplifting . . . with a gleeful zest that's simply irresistible" . . . . Drama Logue

"Fast, fiery, freewheeling . . . sheer dynamism!" . . . . Los Angeles Times

"If only jazz dancing wee always like this!" . . . . Orange County Register

"This concert jazz dance company puts on better shows than most of what one sees on Broadway." . . . . California Magazine

"Definitely the best concert jazz ensemble in L.A.!" . . . . L. A. Weekly

"For taste, style, dancers and longevity, there is probably no other jazz dance company in town that can match Dennon and Sayhber Rawles' Jazz Dancers, Inc." . . . . .Daily Variety

The Rawles' have been commissioned to create numerous works for many High Schools, Colleges and Universities over the years. They include: USC, Orange Coast College, Alan Hancock College, Cal Poly San Luis Obispo, Moorpark College, Riverside College, Cerritos College, Diamond Bar High and Alhambra High.

PUBLISHED WORKS

1984	STAYING FIT - an exercise/fitness book with dance exercises designed by the Rawles' - Published by: Simon and Schuster.

After the release of their 1983 film Staying Alive, starring John Travolta, the Rawles' collaborated with Travolta and personal trainer Dan Isaacson on this exercise/fitness book illustrating the workout program that produced amazing results for the star.

VISIT US AT:
dennonandsayhber.com

OR, LIKE US ON FACEBOOK:
Dennon & Sayhber Rawles

Made in the USA
San Bernardino, CA
09 April 2019